HOW TO USE TH

This flashcard-style book will serve as your guide to learn Spanish quickly and efficiently for your travels or daily needs.

In this book you will find the most commonly used verbs, adjectives, adverbs, and pronouns in the Spanish language.

These "flashcards" are easy to access to help you get out of a "lost in translation" situation efficiently.

Plus, use the index at the back to look up a word within seconds for fast translation.

Let's go!

ABEJA
BEE

ANIMALES - ANIMALS

ARAÑA
SPIDER

ANIMALES - ANIMALS

ÁGUILA
EAGLE

ANIMALES - ANIMALS

ARDILLA
SQUIRREL

ANIMALES - ANIMALS

ARMADILLO

ARMADILLO

BALLENA

WHALE

BUEY

OX

BUITRE

BUZZARD

BURRO
DONKEY

ANIMALES - ANIMALS

BÚHO/LECHUZA
OWL

ANIMALES - ANIMALS

CUCARACHA
COCKROACH

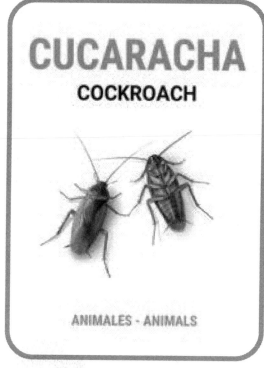

ANIMALES - ANIMALS

CHIVO
GOAT

ANIMALES - ANIMALS

Adriana Muñoz

CABALLO
HORSE

ANIMALES - ANIMALS

CANGURO
KANGAROO

ANIMALES - ANIMALS

CAMELLO
CAMEL

ANIMALES - ANIMALS

CIGÜEÑA
STORK

ANIMALES - ANIMALS

CANGREJO
CRAB

ANIMALES - ANIMALS

CEBRA
ZEBRA

ANIMALES - ANIMALS

CERDO
PIG

ANIMALES - ANIMALS

CIERVO
DEER

ANIMALES - ANIMALS

CONEJO
RABBIT

ANIMALES - ANIMALS

CONDOR
CONDOR

ANIMALES - ANIMALS

COLIBRÍ
HUMMINGBIRD

ANIMALES - ANIMALS

DELFÍN
DOLPHIN

ANIMALES - ANIMALS

ELEFANTE
ELEPHANT

ANIMALES - ANIMALS

ESCARABAJO
BEETLE

ANIMALES - ANIMALS

EMÚ
EMU

ANIMALES - ANIMALS

FLAMENCO
FLAMINGO

ANIMALES - ANIMALS

GATO
CAT

ANIMALES - ANIMALS

GALLINA
HEN

ANIMALES - ANIMALS

GALLO
ROOSTER

ANIMALES - ANIMALS

GOLONDRINA
SWALLOW

ANIMALES - ANIMALS

GAVIOTA
SEAGULL

ANIMALES - ANIMALS

HORMIGA
ANT

ANIMALES - ANIMALS

HIPOPÓTAMO
HIPPOPOTAMUS

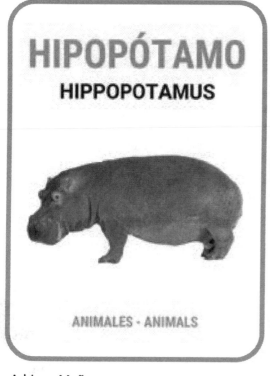

ANIMALES - ANIMALS

JABALÍ
WILD BOAR

ANIMALES - ANIMALS

JIRAFA
GIRAFFE

ANIMALES - ANIMALS

LEÓN
LION

ANIMALES - ANIMALS

LIEBRE
HARE

ANIMALES - ANIMALS

LLAMA
LLAMA

ANIMALES - ANIMALS

MONO
MONKEY

ANIMALES - ANIMALS

MURCIÉLAGO
BAT

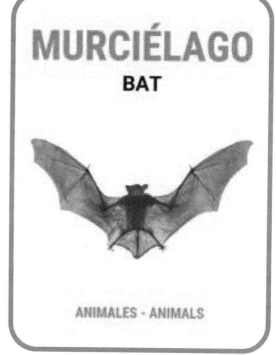

ANIMALES - ANIMALS

MARIPOSA
BUTTERFLY

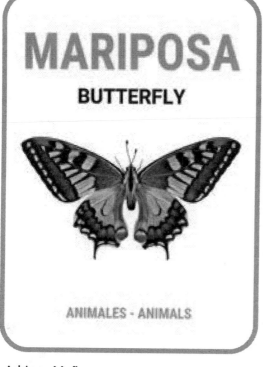

ANIMALES - ANIMALS

OSO
BEAR

ANIMALES - ANIMALS

OVEJA
SHEEP

ANIMALES - ANIMALS

POLLO
CHICKEN

ANIMALES - ANIMALS

PINGÜINO
PENGUIN

ANIMALES - ANIMALS

PUERCO ESPÍN
PORCUPINE

ANIMALES - ANIMALS

PERRO
DOG

ANIMALES - ANIMALS

PEZ
FISH

ANIMALES - ANIMALS

PALOMA
DOVE

ANIMALES - ANIMALS

PAVO
TURKEY

ANIMALES - ANIMALS

PÁJARO
BIRD

ANIMALES - ANIMALS

PAPAGAYO
PARROT

ANIMALES - ANIMALS

RUISEÑOR
NIGHTINGALE

ANIMALES - ANIMALS

RATÓN
MOUSE

ANIMALES - ANIMALS

RANA
FROG

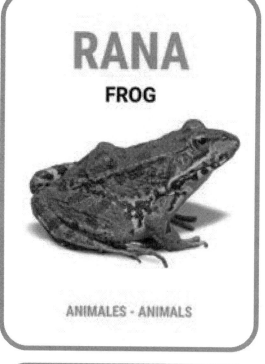

ANIMALES - ANIMALS

SAPO
TOAD

ANIMALES - ANIMALS

SARDINA
SARDINE

ANIMALES - ANIMALS

TORTUGA
TURTLE

ANIMALES - ANIMALS

TORO
BULL

VACA
COW

ZORRO
FOX

DURAZNO
PEACH

SANDÍA
WATERMELON

FRUTAS - FRUITS

MANZANA
APPLE

FRUTAS - FRUITS

CIRUELA
PLUM

FRUTAS - FRUITS

PERA
PEAR

FRUTAS - FRUITS

CEREZA
CHERRY

FRUTAS - FRUITS

BANANA
BANANA

FRUTAS - FRUITS

LIMÓN
LEMON

FRUTAS - FRUITS

UVAS
GRAPES

FRUTAS - FRUITS

NARANJA
ORANGE

FRUTAS - FRUITS

ACEITUNA
OLIVE

FRUTAS - FRUITS

ARÁNDANO
BLUEBERRY

FRUTAS - FRUITS

HIGO
FIG

FRUTAS - FRUITS

FRAMBUESA
RASPBERRY

FRUTAS - FRUITS

MELÓN
MELON

FRUTAS - FRUITS

GRANADA
POMEGRANATE

FRUTAS - FRUITS

CHINOLA
PASSION FRUIT

FRUTAS - FRUITS

PITAYA

PITAYA

FRUTAS - FRUITS

MANGO

MANGO

FRUTAS - FRUITS

PIÑA

PINEAPPLE

FRUTAS - FRUITS

YACA/JACA

JACKFRUIT

FRUTAS - FRUITS

COCO
COCONUT

FRUTAS - FRUITS

GUANABANA
SOURSOP

FRUTAS - FRUITS

CARAMBOLA
CARAMBOLA

FRUTAS - FRUITS

CAQUI
PERSIMMON

FRUTAS - FRUITS

SIDRA

SIDRA

FRUTAS - FRUITS

GUARANÁ

GUARANA

FRUTAS - FRUITS

KIWI

KIWI

FRUTAS - FRUITS

LICHI

LYCHEE

FRUTAS - FRUITS

LIMA
LIME

FRUTAS - FRUITS

NECTARINA
NECTARINE

FRUTAS - FRUITS

PAPAYA
PAPAYA

FRUTAS - FRUITS

TAMARINDO
TAMARIND

FRUTAS - FRUITS

TORONJA
GRAPEFRUIT

FRUTAS - FRUITS

FRUTOS SECOS
NUTS

FRUTAS - FRUITS

NUEZ
WALNUT

FRUTAS - FRUITS

ALMENDRA
KERNELS

FRUTAS - FRUITS

AVELLANA

HAZELNUT

FRUTAS - FRUITS

PISTACHO

PISTACHIO

FRUTAS - FRUITS

PIÑON

PINE NUT

FRUTAS - FRUITS

CASTAÑA

CHESTNUT

FRUTAS - FRUITS

AJO
GARLIC

VERDURAS - VEGETABLES

ACELGA
CHARD

VERDURAS - VEGETABLES

BERENJENA
EGGPLANT

VERDURAS - VEGETABLES

PIMIENTA
PEPPER

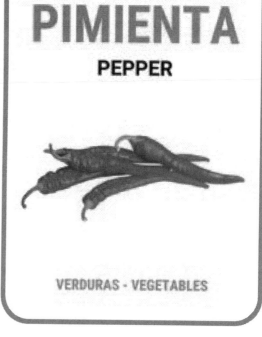

VERDURAS - VEGETABLES

COLIFLOR
CAULIFLOWER

VERDURAS - VEGETABLES

CALABACÍN
ZUCCHINI

VERDURAS - VEGETABLES

TOMATE
TOMATO

VERDURAS - VEGETABLES

PEREJIL
PARSLEY

VERDURAS - VEGETABLES

REPOLLO
CABBAGE

VERDURAS - VEGETABLES

ZANAHORIA
CARROT

VERDURAS - VEGETABLES

ALCACHOFAS
ARTICHOKES

VERDURAS - VEGETABLES

BRÓCOLI
BROCCOLI

VERDURAS - VEGETABLES

PEPINO
CUCUMBER

VERDURAS - VEGETABLES

LECHUGA
LETTUCE

VERDURAS - VEGETABLES

CEBOLLA
ONIONS

VERDURAS - VEGETABLES

FRIJOLES
BEANS

VERDURAS - VEGETABLES

GARBANZO
CHICKPEA

VERDURAS - VEGETABLES

PATATA / PAPAS
POTATO

VERDURAS - VEGETABLES

REMOLACHA
BEET

VERDURAS - VEGETABLES

YUCA
CASSAVA

VERDURAS - VEGETABLES

PIMENTÓN

PARIKA

VERDURAS - VEGETABLES

BERRO

WATERCRESS

VERDURAS - VEGETABLES

CALABAZA

PUMPKIN

VERDURAS - VEGETABLES

APIO

CELERY

VERDURAS - VEGETABLES

ARVEJAS

PEAS

VERDURAS - VEGETABLES

CHOCLO / MAÍZ

CORN

VERDURAS - VEGETABLES

ESPINACA

SPINACH

VERDURAS - VEGETABLES

BLANCO

WHITE

COLORES - COLORS

NEGRO
BLACK

COLORES - COLORS

ROJO
RED

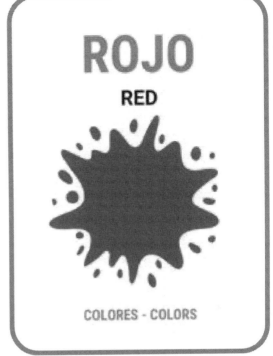

COLORES - COLORS

AMARILLO
YELLLOW

COLORES - COLORS

AZUL
BLUE

COLORES - COLORS

CELESTE
SKY BLUE

COLORES - COLORS

VERDE
GREEN

COLORES - COLORS

BEIGE
LIGHT BROWN

COLORES - COLORS

MORADO
VIOLET

COLORES - COLORS

LILA
PURPLE

COLORES - COLORS

ROSA / ROSADO
PINK

COLORES - COLORS

MARRÓN
BROWN

COLORES - COLORS

GRIS
GREY

COLORES - COLORS

PLATEADO
SILVER

COLORES - COLORS

CREMA
CREAM COLOR

COLORES - COLORS

NARANJA
ORANGE

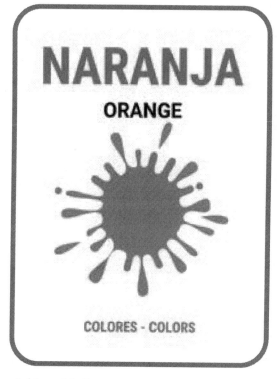

COLORES - COLORS

DORADO
GOLD

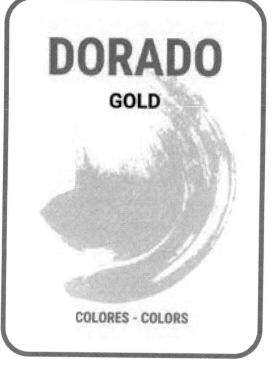

COLORES - COLORS

AFECTUOSO
WARM / LOVING

ADJECTIVOS - ADJECTIVES

AMBICIOSO
AMBITIOUS

ADJECTIVOS - ADJECTIVES

AMABLE
KIND

ADJECTIVOS - ADJECTIVES

HURAÑO
UNSOCIABLE

ADJECTIVOS - ADJECTIVES

ABURRIDO
BORING

ADJECTIVOS - ADJECTIVES

CELOSO
JEALOUS

ADJECTIVOS - ADJECTIVES

ENGREÍDO
SMUG

ADJECTIVOS - ADJECTIVES

VALIENTE
BRAVE

ADJECTIVOS - ADJECTIVES

Adriana Muñoz

CINICO
CYNICAL

TORPE
CLUMSY

DISCRETO
DISCREET / QUIET

DIVERTIDO
FUN

DULCE
SWEET

ADJECTIVOS · ADJECTIVES

EDUCADO
POLITE

ADJECTIVOS · ADJECTIVES

EGOÍSTA
SELFISH

ADJECTIVOS · ADJECTIVES

ELEGANTE
ELEGANT

ADJECTIVOS · ADJECTIVES

Adriana Muñoz

EMPRENDEDOR
ENTREPRENEUR

ADJECTIVOS - ADJECTIVES

ENCANTADOR
CHARMING

ADJECTIVOS - ADJECTIVES

QUISQUILLOSO
PERNICKETY

ADJECTIVOS - ADJECTIVES

EXPERIMENTADO
EXPERIENCED

ADJECTIVOS - ADJECTIVES

FORMAL

FORMAL

ADJECTIVOS - ADJECTIVES

DÉBIL

WEAK

ADJECTIVOS - ADJECTIVES

GENEROSO

GENEROUS

ADJECTIVOS - ADJECTIVES

MALEDUCADO

RUDE

ADJECTIVOS - ADJECTIVES

HÁBIL

SKILLFUL

ADJECTIVOS - ADJECTIVES

INMADURA

IMMATURE

ADJECTIVOS - ADJECTIVES

IMPACIENTE

IMPATIENT

ADJECTIVOS - ADJECTIVES

IMPULSIVO

IMPULSIVE

ADJECTIVOS - ADJECTIVES

INGENUO
NAIVE

INTERESANTE
INTERESTING

INTOLERANTE
INTOLERANT / ILLIBERAL

ENTROMETIDO
MEDDLING

MALHUMURADO

MOODY

ADJECTIVOS - ADJECTIVES

PÍCARO

ROGUE / NAUGHTY

ADJECTIVOS - ADJECTIVES

MALO

BAD / MEAN / EVIL

ADJECTIVOS - ADJECTIVES

METICULOSO

METICULOUS

ADJECTIVOS - ADJECTIVES

MEZQUINO
PETTY

ADJECTIVOS - ADJECTIVES

NERVIOSO
NERVOUS

ADJECTIVOS - ADJECTIVES

ODIOSO
HATEFUL

ADJECTIVOS - ADJECTIVES

PACIENTE
PATIENT

ADJECTIVOS - ADJECTIVES

PERSEVERANTE
PERSISTENT

ADJECTIVOS - ADJECTIVES

PUNTUAL
PROMPT

ADJECTIVOS - ADJECTIVES

PEREZOSO
LAZY

ADJECTIVOS - ADJECTIVES

PRETENCIOSO
PRETENTIOUS

ADJECTIVOS - ADJECTIVES

PROVOCADOR
PROVOCATEUR

ADJECTIVOS · ADJECTIVES

PRUDENTE
PRUDENT

ADJECTIVOS · ADJECTIVES

CASCARRABIAS
CURMUDGEON

ADJECTIVOS · ADJECTIVES

RESPONSABLE
RESPONSIBLE

ADJECTIVOS · ADJECTIVES

DURO
STRONG

BARATO
CHEAP

RIDÍCULO
RIDICULOUS

SEGURO
SAFE

SENSATO
WISE / RATIONAL

ADJECTIVOS - ADJECTIVES

SENSIBLE
SENSITIVE

ADJECTIVOS - ADJECTIVES

SIMPÁTICO
NICE / FRIENDLY

ADJECTIVOS - ADJECTIVES

SINCERO
HONEST

ADJECTIVOS - ADJECTIVES

SUCIO
DIRTY

ADJECTIVOS - ADJECTIVES

SUPERFICIAL
SHALLOW PERSON

ADJECTIVOS - ADJECTIVES

TRAVIESO
NAUGHTY

ADJECTIVOS - ADJECTIVES

TRISTE
SAD

ADJECTIVOS - ADJECTIVES

TÍMIDO
SHY

CALIENTE
HOT

FEO
UGLY

GUAPO
HANDSOME

FUERTE
STRONG

PEQUEÑO
SMALL

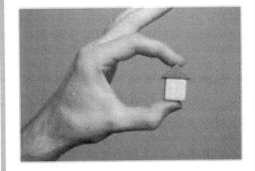

GRANDE
BIG

CORTÉS
POLITE

NOBLE
HONORABLE

ADJECTIVOS · ADJECTIVES

VANIDOSO
VAIN

ADJECTIVOS · ADJECTIVES

CRUEL
CRUEL

ADJECTIVOS · ADJECTIVES

DÉBIL
WEAK

ADJECTIVOS · ADJECTIVES

FELIZ
HAPPY

ADJECTIVOS - ADJECTIVES

FLACO
SKINNY

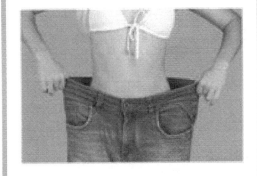

ADJECTIVOS - ADJECTIVES

GORDO
FAT

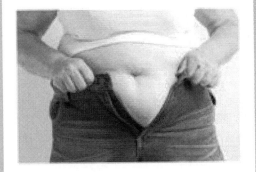

ADJECTIVOS - ADJECTIVES

RUBIO
BLOND

ADJECTIVOS - ADJECTIVES

MORENO
DARK SKIN

ADJECTIVOS · ADJECTIVES

VIEJO
OLD

ADJECTIVOS · ADJECTIVES

NUEVO
NEW

ADJECTIVOS · ADJECTIVES

SIMPLE
SIMPLE

ADJECTIVOS · ADJECTIVES

Adriana Muñoz

RARO

ODD

ADJECTIVOS - ADJECTIVES

ALEMÁN / ALEMANA

GERMAN

ADJECTIVOS - ADJECTIVES

CANADIENSE

CANADIAN

ADJECTIVOS - ADJECTIVES

CHINO/A

CHINESE

ADJECTIVOS - ADJECTIVES

ESPAÑOL / ESPAÑOLA
SPANISH

ADJECTIVOS - ADJECTIVES

ESTADOUNIDENSE
AMERICAN

ADJECTIVOS - ADJECTIVES

FRANCÉS / FRANCESA
FRENCH

ADJECTIVOS - ADJECTIVES

HAITIANO/A
HAITIAN

ADJECTIVOS - ADJECTIVES

INGLÉS / INGLESA
ENGLISH

ADJECTIVOS - ADJECTIVES

ITALIANO / A
ITALIAN

ADJECTIVOS - ADJECTIVES

JAMAICANO / A
JAMAICAN

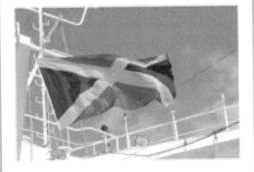

ADJECTIVOS - ADJECTIVES

JAPONÉS / JAPONESA
JAPANESE

ADJECTIVOS - ADJECTIVES

MEXICANO / A
MEXICAN

ADJECTIVOS - ADJECTIVES

PUERTORRIQUEÑO / A
PUERTO RICAN

ADJECTIVOS - ADJECTIVES

DOMINICANO / A
DOMINICAN REPUBLIC

ADJECTIVOS - ADJECTIVES

RUSO / A
RUSSIAN

ADJECTIVOS - ADJECTIVES

BRASILEÑO / A

BRAZILIAN

PORTUGUÉS / PORTUGUESA

PORTUGUESE

ADJECTIVOS · ADJECTIVES

CAFÉ

COFFEE

SUBSTANTIVOS · NOUNS

LIBRO

BOOK

SUBSTANTIVOS · NOUNS

MARTILLO
HAMMER

SUBSTANTIVOS - NOUNS

ESTRELLA
STAR

SUBSTANTIVOS - NOUNS

LETRAS
LETTERS

SUBSTANTIVOS - NOUNS

MENSAJES
MESSAGES

SUBSTANTIVOS - NOUNS

Adriana Muñoz

COLEGIO

SCHOOL

SUBSTANTIVOS - NOUNS

ISLA

ISLAND

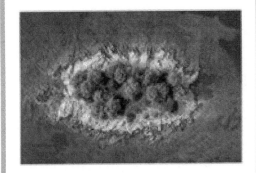

SUBSTANTIVOS - NOUNS

MÚSICO

MUSICIAN

SUBSTANTIVOS - NOUNS

SOLDADO

SOLDIER

SUBSTANTIVOS - NOUNS

BOSQUE
WOODS

SUBSTANTIVOS - NOUNS

FAUNA
WILDLIFE

SUBSTANTIVOS - NOUNS

LATA
CAN

SUBSTANTIVOS - NOUNS

OJOS
EYES

SUBSTANTIVOS - NOUNS

PIE
TOE

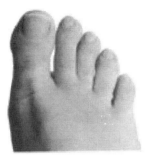

SUBSTANTIVOS - NOUNS

CABEZA
HEAD

SUBSTANTIVOS - NOUNS

MANO
HAND

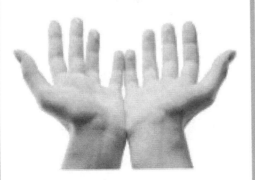

SUBSTANTIVOS - NOUNS

CUELLO
NECK

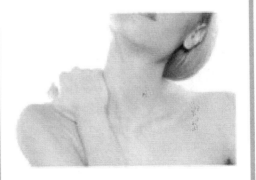

SUBSTANTIVOS - NOUNS

CABELLO
HAIR

SUBSTANTIVOS - NOUNS

NARIZ
NOSE

SUBSTANTIVOS - NOUNS

BOCA
MOUTH

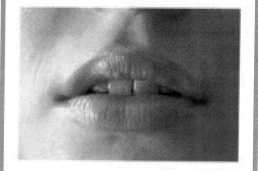

SUBSTANTIVOS - NOUNS

DEDOS
FINGERS

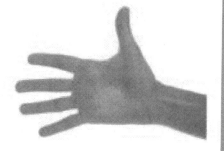

SUBSTANTIVOS - NOUNS

UÑAS
NAILS

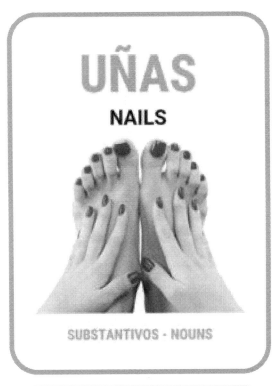

SUBSTANTIVOS · NOUNS

PIEL
SKIN

SUBSTANTIVOS · NOUNS

CINTURA
WAIST

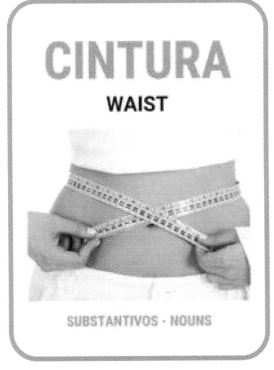

SUBSTANTIVOS · NOUNS

CADERA
HIP

SUBSTANTIVOS · NOUNS

CEPILLO DE DIENTES
TOOTHBRUSH

SUBSTANTIVOS · NOUNS

PEINE
COMB HAIR

SUBSTANTIVOS · NOUNS

BAGAJE
BAGGAGE

SUBSTANTIVOS · NOUNS

ABRELATAS
CAN OPENER

SUBSTANTIVOS · NOUNS

PARAGUAS
UMBRELLA

ROMPECABEZAS
PUZZLE

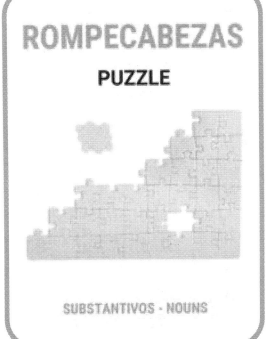

SALVAVIDAS
LIFEGUARD

ANTEOJO
GLASSES

CAMA
BED

SUBSTANTIVOS · NOUNS

PUERTA
DOOR

SUBSTANTIVOS · NOUNS

HOJAS
LEAF

SUBSTANTIVOS · NOUNS

CUCHILLO
KNIFE

SUBSTANTIVOS · NOUNS

Adriana Muñoz

CARAMELO
CANDY

CUCHARA
SPOON

TENEDOR
FORK

RUEDA
WHEEL

HERRAMIENTA
TOOL

SUBSTANTIVOS · NOUNS

ARTE
ART

SUBSTANTIVOS · NOUNS

AGUA
WATER

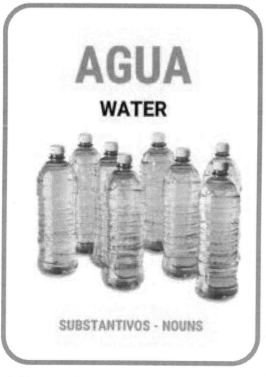

SUBSTANTIVOS · NOUNS

TELÉFONO
PHONE

SUBSTANTIVOS · NOUNS

Adriana Muñoz

ARTESANO

CRAFTSMAN

SUBSTANTIVOS - NOUNS

NIÑEZ

CHILDHOOD

SUBSTANTIVOS - NOUNS

CABALLERO

GENTLEMAN / KNIGHT

SUBSTANTIVOS - NOUNS

PELAJE

FUR

SUBSTANTIVOS - NOUNS

MUJER

WOMAN

MUJERES: WOMEN

SUBSTANTIVOS · NOUNS

HOMBRE

MAN

HOMBRES: MEN

SUBSTANTIVOS · NOUNS

ROPA

CLOTHES

SUBSTANTIVOS · NOUNS

CIUDAD

CITY

SUBSTANTIVOS · NOUNS

AVIÓN
AIRPLANE

SUBSTANTIVOS · NOUNS

CAMIÓN
TRUCK

SUBSTANTIVOS · NOUNS

AUTO
CAR

SUBSTANTIVOS · NOUNS

AUTOBÚS
BUS

SUBSTANTIVOS · NOUNS

Speak Spanish Like A Native

HELICÓPTERO
HELICOPTER

SUBSTANTIVOS · NOUNS

BICICLETA
BICYCLE/BIKE

SUBSTANTIVOS · NOUNS

METRO
SUBWAY

SUBSTANTIVOS · NOUNS

PARACHOQUES
BUMPER

SUBSTANTIVOS · NOUNS

CLIMA
WEATHER

SUBSTANTIVOS - NOUNS

MAPA
MAP

SUBSTANTIVOS - NOUNS

PLANETA
PLANET

SUBSTANTIVOS - NOUNS

IDIOMA
LANGUAGE

SUBSTANTIVOS - NOUNS

LUNES
MONDAY

SUBSTANTIVOS · NOUNS

MARTES
TUESDAY

SUBSTANTIVOS · NOUNS

MIÉRCOLES
WEDNESDAY

SUBSTANTIVOS · NOUNS

JUEVES
THURSDAY

SUBSTANTIVOS · NOUNS

VIERNES

FRIDAY

SUBSTANTIVOS · NOUNS

SÁBADO

SATURDAY

SUBSTANTIVOS · NOUNS

DOMINGO

SUNDAY

SUBSTANTIVOS · NOUNS

CUMPLEAÑOS

BIRTHDAY

SUBSTANTIVOS · NOUNS

DUCHA
SHOWER

SUBSTANTIVOS · NOUNS

HELADERA
FRIDGE

SUBSTANTIVOS · NOUNS

HORNO
OVEN

SUBSTANTIVOS · NOUNS

BALCÓN
BALCONY

SUBSTANTIVOS · NOUNS

NIÑO
BOY

SUBSTANTIVOS · NOUNS

NIÑA
GIRL

SUBSTANTIVOS · NOUNS

LÁPIS
PENCIL

SUBSTANTIVOS · NOUNS

TIJERA
SCISSORS

SUBSTANTIVOS · NOUNS

RASCACIELOS
SKYSCRAPERS

SUBSTANTIVOS · NOUNS

TIERRA
EARTH

SUBSTANTIVOS · NOUNS

SILLA
CHAIR

SUBSTANTIVOS · NOUNS

OJOTAS
FLIP-FLOPS

SUBSTANTIVOS · NOUNS

ZAPATO

SHOES

SUBSTANTIVOS - NOUNS

GUARDARROPA

CLOSET

SUBSTANTIVOS - NOUNS

CORAZÓN

HEART

SUBSTANTIVOS - NOUNS

VIAJE

TRIP

SUBSTANTIVOS - NOUNS

TAXISTA
CAB DRIVER

SUBSTANTIVOS · NOUNS

EQUIPAJE
LUGGAGE

SUBSTANTIVOS · NOUNS

CARTA
LETTER

SUBSTANTIVOS · NOUNS

BOLÍGRAFO
PEN

SUBSTANTIVOS · NOUNS

GOMA
RUBBER

SUBSTANTIVOS - NOUNS

AMOR
LOVE

SUBSTANTIVOS - NOUNS

QUESO
CHEESE

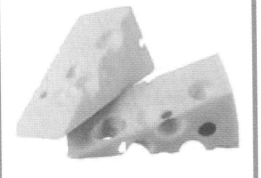

COMIDA - MEAL

PAN
BREAD

COMIDA - MEAL

HARINA
FLOUR

COMIDA - MEAL

ARROZ
RICE

COMIDA - MEAL

PASTA
PASTA

COMIDA - MEAL

HUEVO
EGG

COMIDA - MEAL

MIEL
HONEY

COMIDA - MEAL

AZÚCAR
SUGAR

COMIDA - MEAL

SAL
SALT

COMIDA - MEAL

MERMELADA
JAM

COMIDA - MEAL

YOGUR
YOGURT

COMIDA - MEAL

AVENA
OAT

COMIDA - MEAL

HAMBURGUESA
HAMBURGER / BURGER

COMIDA - MEAL

PIZZA
PIZZA

COMIDA - MEAL

PANCHO / PERRITO CALIENTE
HOTDOG

COMIDA - MEAL

SOPA
SOUP

COMIDA - MEAL

ENSALADA
SALAD

COMIDA - MEAL

PAPAS FRITAS
FRIES / POTATO CHIPS

COMIDA - MEAL

SÁNDWICHES
SANDWICH

COMIDA - MEAL

PALOMITAS
POPCORN

COMIDA - MEAL

NACHOS
NACHOS

COMIDA - MEAL

TACOS
TACOS

COMIDA - MEAL

BOCADILLO

SNACK

COMIDA - MEAL

CARNE

MEAT

COMIDA - MEAL

BIFE

MEAT / BEEF

COMIDA - MEAL

CERVEZA

BEER

COMIDA - MEAL

AGUA
WATER

COMIDA - MEAL

RESFRESCOS
SOFT DRINKS

COMIDA - MEAL

CAFÉ
COFFEE

COMIDA - MEAL

LECHE
MILK

COMIDA - MEAL

EL BATIDO

MILKSHAKE

COMIDA - MEAL

JUGO

JUICE

COMIDA - MEAL

TÉ

TEA

COMIDA - MEAL

TORTA

CAKE

COMIDA - MEAL

JAMON
HAM

COMIDA - MEAL

VINO
WINE

COMIDA - MEAL

AZEITE DE OLIVA
OLIVE OIL

COMIDA - MEAL

MANTEQUILLA
BUTTER

COMIDA - MEAL

GUACAMOLE

GUACAMOLE

COMIDA - MEAL

SURGIR/ LEVANTARSE

ARISE

VERBOS - VERBS

DESPERTARSE

AWAKE

VERBOS - VERBS

SER / ESTAR

BE / AM , ARE, IS

VERBOS - VERBS

SOPORTAR
BEAR

VERBOS - VERBS

GOLPEAR
BEAT / HIT / STRIKE

VERBOS - VERBS

LLEGAR A SER
BECAME

VERBOS - VERBS

EMPEZAR
BEGIN

VERBOS - VERBS

DOBLAR
BEND

VERBOS - VERBS

APOSTAR
BET

VERBOS - VERBS

ATAR
BIND

VERBOS - VERBS

PUJAR
BID

VERBOS - VERBS

MORDER
BITE

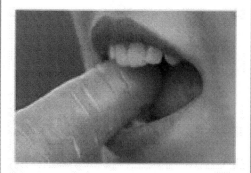

VERBOS - VERBS

SANGRAR
BLEED

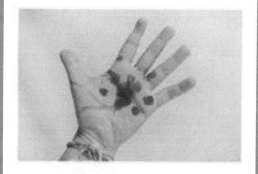

VERBOS - VERBS

SOPLAR
BLOW

VERBOS - VERBS

ROMPER
BREAK

VERBOS - VERBS

CRIAR
BREED

VERBOS · VERBS

TRAER / LLEVAR
BRING

VERBOS · VERBS

RADIAR
BROADCAST

VERBOS · VERBS

EDIFICAR
BUILD

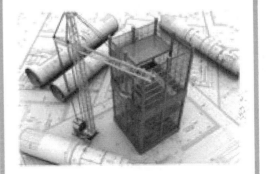

VERBOS · VERBS

QUEMAR
BURN

VERBOS - VERBS

REVENTAR
BURST

VERBOS - VERBS

COMPRAR
BUY

VERBOS - VERBS

ARROJAR
CAST

VERBOS - VERBS

COGER
CATCH

VENIR
COME

COSTAR
COST

CORTAR
CUT

ELIGER
CHOOSE

VERBOS - VERBS

AGARRARSE
CLING

VERBOS - VERBS

ARRASTARSE
CREEP

VERBOS - VERBS

TRATAR
DEAL

VERBOS - VERBS

CAVAR
DIG

VERBOS - VERBS

HACER
DO / DOES

VERBOS - VERBS

DIBUJAR
DRAW

VERBOS - VERBS

SOÑAR
DREAM

VERBOS - VERBS

BEBER
DRINK

VERBOS - VERBS

CONDUCIR
DRIVE

VERBOS - VERBS

COMER
EAT

VERBOS - VERBS

CAER
FALL

VERBOS - VERBS

Adriana Muñoz

ALIMENTAR
FEED

VERBOS - VERBS

SENTIR
FEEL

VERBOS - VERBS

LUCHAR
FIGHT

VERBOS - VERBS

ENCONTRAR
FIND

VERBOS - VERBS

Speak Spanish Like A Native

HUIR
FLEE

VERBOS · VERBS

VOLAR
FLY

VERBOS · VERBS

PROHIBIR
FORBID

VERBOS · VERBS

OLVIDAR
FORGOT

VERBOS · VERBS

PERDONAR
FORGIVE

VERBOS - VERBS

HELAR
FREEZE

VERBOS - VERBS

OBTENER
GET

VERBOS - VERBS

DAR
GIVE

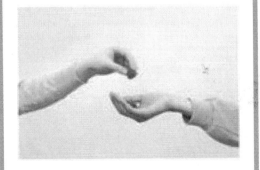

VERBOS - VERBS

IR
GO / GOES

VERBOS - VERBS

CRECER
GROW

VERBOS - VERBS

MOLER
GRIND

VERBOS - VERBS

COLGAR
HANG

VERBOS - VERBS

Adriana Muñoz

HABER / TENER
HAVE

VERBOS - VERBS

OIR
HEAR

VERBOS - VERBS

OCULTAR
HIDE

VERBOS - VERBS

AGARRAR
HOLD

VERBOS - VERBS

HERIR
HURT

VERBOS - VERBS

CONSERVAR
KEEP

VERBOS - VERBS

SABER / CONOCER
KNOW

VERBOS - VERBS

ARRODILLARSE
KNEEL

VERBOS - VERBS

HACER PUNTO

KNIT

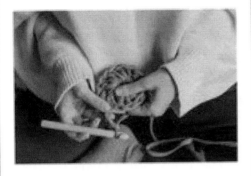

VERBOS - VERBS

PONER

LAY

VERBOS - VERBS

CONDUCIR

LEAD

VERBOS - VERBS

APOYARSE

LEAN

VERBOS - VERBS

BRINCAR
LEAP

VERBOS - VERBS

APRENDER
LEARN

VERBOS - VERBS

DEJAR
LEAVE

VERBOS - VERBS

PRESTAR
LEND

VERBOS - VERBS

Adriana Muñoz

PERMITIR
LET

VERBOS - VERBS

ECHARSE
LIE

VERBOS - VERBS

ENCENDER
LIGHT

VERBOS - VERBS

PERDER
LOSE

VERBOS - VERBS

HACER
MAKE

VERBOS · VERBS

SIGNIFICAR
MEAN

VERBOS · VERBS

ENCONTRAR
MEET

VERBOS · VERBS

EQUIVOCAR
MISTAKE

VERBOS · VERBS

VENCER
OVERCOME

VERBOS - VERBS

PAGAR
PAY

VERBOS - VERBS

PONER
PUT

VERBOS - VERBS

LEER
READ

VERBOS - VERBS

MONTAR

RIDE

VERBOS - VERBS

LLAMAR

RING / CALL

VERBOS - VERBS

LEVANTARSE

RISE

VERBOS - VERBS

CORRER

RUN

VERBOS - VERBS

DECIR
SAY

VERBOS · VERBS

VER
SEE

VERBOS · VERBS

BUSCAR
SEEK

VERBOS · VERBS

VENDER
SELL

VERBOS · VERBS

ENVIAR
SEND

VERBOS - VERBS

PONER (SE)
SET

VERBOS - VERBS

COSER
SEW

VERBOS - VERBS

SACUDIR
SHAKE

VERBOS - VERBS

ESQUILAR
SHEAR

VERBOS - VERBS

BRILLAR
SHINE

VERBOS - VERBS

DISPARAR
SHOOT

VERBOS - VERBS

MOSTRAR
SHOW

VERBOS - VERBS

ENCOGERSE
SHRINK

VERBOS · VERBS

CERRAR
SHUT

VERBOS · VERBS

CANTAR
SING

VERBOS · VERBS

HUNDIR
SINK

VERBOS · VERBS

Adriana Muñoz

SENTARSE

SIT

VERBOS - VERBS

DORMIR

SLEEP

VERBOS - VERBS

RESBALAR

SLIDE

VERBOS - VERBS

OLER

SMELL

VERBOS - VERBS

SEMBRAR
SOW

VERBOS - VERBS

HABLAR
SPEAK / TALK

VERBOS - VERBS

ACELERAR
SPEED

VERBOS - VERBS

DELETREAR
SPELL

VERBOS - VERBS

GASTAR
SPEND

VERBOS - VERBS

DERRAMAR
SPILL

VERBOS - VERBS

HILAR
SPIN

VERBOS - VERBS

ESCUPIR
SPIT

VERBOS - VERBS

HENDER / PARTIR / RAJAR

SPLIT

VERBOS - VERBS

ENTROPEAR

SPOIL

VERBOS - VERBS

EXTENDER

SPREAD

VERBOS - VERBS

SALTAR

SPRING

VERBOS - VERBS

ESTAR EN PIE
STAND

VERBOS - VERBS

ROBAR
STEAL

VERBOS - VERBS

PEGAR / ENGOMAR
STICK

VERBOS - VERBS

PICAR
STING

VERBOS - VERBS

APESTAR
STINK

VERBOS - VERBS

DAR ZANCADAS
STRIDE

VERBOS - VERBS

JURAR
SWEAR

VERBOS - VERBS

SUDAR
SWEAT

VERBOS - VERBS

BARRER
SWEEP

VERBOS · VERBS

HINCHAR
SWELL

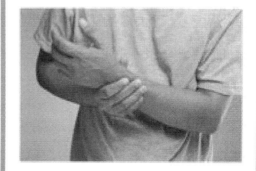

VERBOS · VERBS

NADAR
SWIM

VERBOS · VERBS

COLUMPIARSE
SWING

VERBOS · VERBS

COGER
TAKE

VERBOS - VERBS

ENSEÑAR
TEACH

VERBOS - VERBS

RASGAR
TEAR

VERBOS - VERBS

DECIR
TELL

VERBOS - VERBS

PENSAR
THINK

VERBOS - VERBS

ARRONJAR / TIRAR
THROW

VERBOS - VERBS

INTRODUCIR
THRUST

VERBOS - VERBS

PISAR / HOLLAR
TREAD

VERBOS - VERBS

ENTENDER
UNDERSTAND

VERBOS - VERBS

SUFRIR
SUFFER / UNDERGO

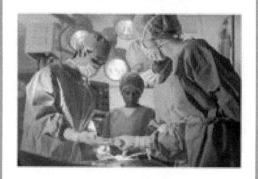

VERBOS - VERBS

EMPRENDER
UNDERTAKE

VERBOS - VERBS

DESPERTARSE
WAKE

VERBOS - VERBS

PONERSE
WEAR

VERBOS - VERBS

TEJER
WEAVE

VERBOS - VERBS

LLORAR
WEEP / CRY

VERBOS - VERBS

MOJAR
WET

VERBOS - VERBS

GANAR
WIN / EARN / GAIN

VERBOS - VERBS

ENROLLAR
WIND

VERBOS - VERBS

RETIRARSE
WITHDRAW

VERBOS - VERBS

TORCER
WRING

VERBOS - VERBS

ESCRIBIR
WRITE

VERBOS · VERBS

ABANDONAR
ABANDON

VERBOS · VERBS

ABSOLVER
ABSOLVE

VERBOS · VERBS

INJURIAR
ABUSE

VERBOS · VERBS

ACELERAR

ACCELERATE

VERBOS - VERBS

ACEPTAR

ACCEPT

VERBOS - VERBS

ACOSTUMBRAR

ACCUSTOM

VERBOS - VERBS

ADQUIRIR

ACQUIRE

VERBOS - VERBS

SUMAR
ADD

VERBOS - VERBS

ADMIRAR
ADMIRE

VERBOS - VERBS

ADORAR
ADORE

VERBOS - VERBS

AVANZAR
ADVANCE

VERBOS - VERBS

ACONSEJAR

ADVISE

VERBOS - VERBS

ACCEDER

AGREE

VERBOS - VERBS

ASCENDER

AMOUNT

VERBOS - VERBS

ANUNCIAR

ANNOUNCE

VERBOS - VERBS

CONTESTAR
ANSWER

VERBOS - VERBS

APARECER
APPEAR

VERBOS - VERBS

ACERCARSE
APPROACH

VERBOS - VERBS

ARREGLAR
ARRANGE

VERBOS - VERBS

PREGUNTAR

ASK

VERBOS - VERBS

ASOMBRAR

ASTONISH

VERBOS - VERBS

INTENTAR

ATTEMPT

VERBOS - VERBS

ATRAER

ATTRACT

VERBOS - VERBS

BAÑARSE

BATHE

VERBOS · VERBS

CREER

BELIEVE

VERBOS · VERBS

CULPAR

BLAME

VERBOS · VERBS

COBRAR

CASH

VERBOS · VERBS

CAMBIAR
CHANGE

VERBOS - VERBS

RECLAMAR
CLAIM

VERBOS - VERBS

ACLARAR
CLEAR

VERBOS - VERBS

LIMPIAR
CLEAN UP

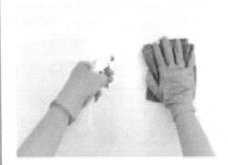

VERBOS - VERBS

CERRAR
CLOSE

VERBOS - VERBS

PEINAR
COMB

VERBOS - VERBS

COMPARAR
COMPARE

VERBOS - VERBS

MANDAR
COMMAND

VERBOS - VERBS

COMPONER

COMPOSE

VERBOS - VERBS

CONSIDERAR

CONSIDER

VERBOS - VERBS

CONTENER

CONTAIN

VERBOS - VERBS

COPIAR

COPY

VERBOS - VERBS

TOSER
COUGH

VERBOS - VERBS

CUBRIR
COVER

VERBOS - VERBS

CORONAR
CROWN

VERBOS - VERBS

DAÑAR
DAMAGE

VERBOS - VERBS

AMANECER

DAWN

VERBOS - VERBS

EMPLEAR

EMPLOY

VERBOS - VERBS

ANIMAR

ENCOURAGE

VERBOS - VERBS

LLEGAR

ARRIVE

VERBOS - VERBS

DECIDIR
DECIDE

VERBOS - VERBS

DEFENDER
DEFEND

VERBOS - VERBS

DESEAR
DESIRE

VERBOS - VERBS

DESTRUIR
DESTROY

VERBOS - VERBS

DESARROLLAR
DEVELOP

VERBOS - VERBS

DEVORAR
DEVOUR

VERBOS - VERBS

DESAPROBAR
DISLIKE

VERBOS - VERBS

DIVIDIR
DIVIDE

VERBOS - VERBS

DEJAR CAER
DROP

VERBOS - VERBS

DISFRUTAR
ENJOY

VERBOS - VERBS

ESTABLECER
ESTABLISH

VERBOS - VERBS

EVOCAR
EVOKE

VERBOS - VERBS

ESPERAR
EXPECT / WAIT

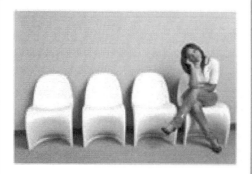

VERBOS - VERBS

ESTALLAR
EXPLODE

VERBOS - VERBS

EXPRESAR
EXPRESS

VERBOS - VERBS

FALLAR
FAIL

VERBOS - VERBS

IR POR
FETCH

VERBOS - VERBS

ACABAR
FINISH

VERBOS - VERBS

AJUSTAR
FIT

VERBOS - VERBS

FLOTAR
FLOAT

VERBOS - VERBS

SEGUIR

FOLLOW

VERBOS - VERBS

RECOGER

GATHER

VERBOS - VERBS

CONCEDER

GRANT

VERBOS - VERBS

GUARDAR

GUARD

VERBOS - VERBS

MANEJAR
HANDLE

VERBOS - VERBS

SUCEDER
HAPPEN

VERBOS - VERBS

CALENTAR
HEAT

VERBOS - VERBS

ALQUILAR
HIRE / RENT

VERBOS - VERBS

CAZAR
HUNT

VERBOS - VERBS

IMAGINAR
IMAGINE

VERBOS - VERBS

IMPORTAR
IMPORT

VERBOS - VERBS

MEJORAR
IMPROVE

VERBOS - VERBS

AUMENTAR
INCREASE

VERBOS - VERBS

PROPONERSE
INTEND

VERBOS - VERBS

INVITAR
INVITE

VERBOS - VERBS

UNIR
JOIN / UNITE

VERBOS - VERBS

SALTAR
JUMP

VERBOS - VERBS

COCEAR
KICK

VERBOS - VERBS

BESAR
KISS

VERBOS - VERBS

ATERRIZAR
LAND

VERBOS - VERBS

REÍR
LAUGH

VERBOS - VERBS

GUSTAR
LIKE

VERBOS - VERBS

VIVIR
LIVE

VERBOS - VERBS

AMAR
LOVE

VERBOS - VERBS

MANTENER
MAINTAIN / KEEP

VERBOS - VERBS

MEDIR
MEASURE

VERBOS - VERBS

MENCIONAR
MENTION

VERBOS - VERBS

NOMBRAR
NAME

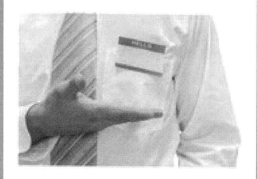

VERBOS - VERBS

NOTAR

NOTICE

VERBOS - VERBS

OBEDECER

OBEY

VERBOS - VERBS

OBLIGAR

OBLIGE

VERBOS - VERBS

OFRECER

OFFER

VERBOS - VERBS

Speak Spanish Like A Native

ORDENAR

ORDER

VERBOS - VERBS

EMPAQUETAR

PACK

VERBOS - VERBS

PASAR

PASS

VERBOS - VERBS

COLOCAR

PLACE

VERBOS - VERBS

AGRADAR
PLEASE

VERBOS - VERBS

PRACTICAR
PRACTISE

VERBOS - VERBS

PREPARAR
PREPARE

VERBOS - VERBS

PRODUCIR
PRODUCE

VERBOS - VERBS

PROPONER
PROPOSE

VERBOS - VERBS

CASTIGAR
PUNISH

VERBOS - VERBS

LLOVER
RAIN

VERBOS - VERBS

RECIBIR
RECEIVE

VERBOS - VERBS

Adriana Muñoz

REHUSAR
REFUSE

VERBOS - VERBS

PERMANECER
REMAIN

VERBOS - VERBS

RECORDAR
REMIND

VERBOS - VERBS

ARRENDAR
RENT

VERBOS - VERBS

REPETIR
REPEAT

VERBOS - VERBS

INFORMAR
REPORT

VERBOS - VERBS

REQUERIR
REQUIRE

VERBOS - VERBS

VOLVER
RETURN

VERBOS - VERBS

NAVEGAR
SAIL

VERBOS · VERBS

PARECER
SEEM

VERBOS · VERBS

GRITAR
SHOUT

VERBOS · VERBS

SONREÍR
SMILE

VERBOS · VERBS

SONAR
SOUND

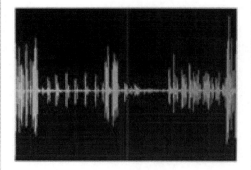

VERBOS - VERBS

PARAR
STOP

VERBOS - VERBS

SUPONER
SUPPOSE

VERBOS - VERBS

PROBAR
TASTE / TRY

VERBOS - VERBS

TOCAR
TOUCH

VERBOS - VERBS

AGRADECER
THANK

VERBOS - VERBS

TRADUCIR
TRANSLATE

VERBOS - VERBS

MOLESTAR
ANNOY / TROUBLE

VERBOS - VERBS

VARIAR
VARY

VERBOS - VERBS

QUERER
WANT

VERBOS - VERBS

VIGILAR
WATCH

VERBOS - VERBS

DESEAR
WISH

VERBOS - VERBS

PREOCUPARSE

WORRY

VERBOS · VERBS

ABOLIR

ABOLISH

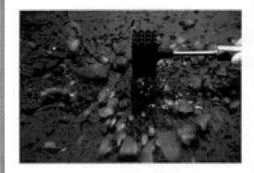

VERBOS · VERBS

ABSORBER

ABSORB

VERBOS · VERBS

ACCEDER

AGREE

VERBOS · VERBS

ACENTUAR
ACCENT

VERBOS - VERBS

ACUSAR
ACCUSE

VERBOS - VERBS

CONSEGUIR
ACHIEVE

VERBOS - VERBS

ACTUAR
ACT

VERBOS - VERBS

DIRIGIR
DRIVE

VERBOS - VERBS

ADMITIR
ADMIT

VERBOS - VERBS

ADORNAR
DECORATE

VERBOS - VERBS

ANUNCIAR
ADVERTISE

VERBOS - VERBS

AFIRMAR
AFFIRM

VERBOS - VERBS

PERMITIR
ALLOW

VERBOS - VERBS

DIVERTIR
AMUSE / HAVE FUN

VERBOS - VERBS

EXCUSARSE
APOLOGIZE

VERBOS - VERBS

NOMBRAR

APPOINT

VERBOS - VERBS

APROBAR

APPROVE

VERBOS - VERBS

ASEGURAR

ASSURE

VERBOS - VERBS

ATACAR

ATTACK

VERBOS - VERBS

ASISTIR
ATTEND / WATCH

VERBOS - VERBS

EVITAR
AVOID

VERBOS - VERBS

ROGAR / PEDIR
BEG

VERBOS - VERBS

PERTENECER
BELONG

VERBOS - VERBS

RESERVAR
BOOK

VERBOS - VERBS

LLEVAR
CARRY

VERBOS - VERBS

CESAR
CEASE

VERBOS - VERBS

COMPROBAR
CHECK

VERBOS - VERBS

LIMPIAR
CLEAN

VERBOS - VERBS

TREPAR
CLIMB

VERBOS - VERBS

RECOGER
COLLECT

VERBOS - VERBS

COMBINAR
COMBINE

VERBOS - VERBS

COMETER
COMMIT

VERBOS - VERBS

QUEJARSE
COMPLAIN

VERBOS - VERBS

OCULTAR
CONCEAL

VERBOS - VERBS

CONSISTIR
CONSIST

VERBOS - VERBS

CONTINUAR
CONTINUE

VERBOS - VERBS

CORREGIR
CORRECT

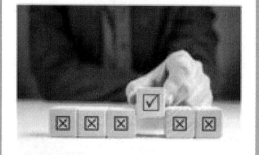

VERBOS - VERBS

CONTAR
COUNT

VERBOS - VERBS

CRUZAR
CROSS

VERBOS - VERBS

BAILAR
DANCE

VERBOS - VERBS

ENGAÑAR
DECEIVE

VERBOS - VERBS

DECLARAR
DECLARE

VERBOS - VERBS

ENTREGAR
DELIVER

VERBOS - VERBS

DESPRECIAR

DESPISE

VERBOS - VERBS

SEPARAR

DETACH

VERBOS - VERBS

DESCUBRIR

DISCOVER

VERBOS - VERBS

DEDICAR

DEVOTE

VERBOS - VERBS

Adriana Muñoz

PERTURBAR

DISTURB

VERBOS - VERBS

ARRASTRAR

DRAG

VERBOS - VERBS

SECAR

DRY

VERBOS - VERBS

INCLUIR

ENCLOSE

VERBOS - VERBS

TERMINAR
END

VERBOS - VERBS

ENTRAR
ENTER

VERBOS - VERBS

ESTIMAR
ESTEEM

VERBOS - VERBS

CAMBIAR
EXCHANGE

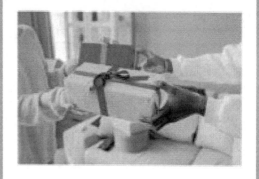

VERBOS - VERBS

EXPLICAR
EXPLAIN

VERBOS - VERBS

EXPONER
EXPOSE

VERBOS - VERBS

EXTRAER
EXTRACT

VERBOS - VERBS

LLENAR
FILL

VERBOS - VERBS

PESCAR

FISH

VERBOS - VERBS

FIJAR

FIX

VERBOS - VERBS

DOBLAR

FOLD

VERBOS - VERBS

FUNDAR

FOUND

VERBOS - VERBS

JUGAR
GAMBLE / PLAY

VERBOS - VERBS

GOVERNAR
GOVERN

VERBOS - VERBS

SALUDAR
GREET

VERBOS - VERBS

ADIVINAR
GUESS

VERBOS - VERBS

AHORCAR
HANG

VERBOS - VERBS

ODIAR
HATE

VERBOS - VERBS

AYUDAR
HELP

VERBOS - VERBS

APRESURARSE
HURRY

VERBOS - VERBS

Adriana Muñoz

IMPLICAR
IMPLY

VERBOS - VERBS

IMPRESIONAR
IMPRESS

VERBOS - VERBS

INCLUIR
INCLUDE

VERBOS - VERBS

AVERIGUAR
INQUIRE

VERBOS - VERBS

INVENTAR
INVENT

VERBOS - VERBS

PLANCHAR
IRON

VERBOS - VERBS

BROMEAR
JOKE

VERBOS - VERBS

JUSTIFICAR
JUSTIFY

VERBOS - VERBS

MATAR
KILL

VERBOS - VERBS

DURAR
LAST

VERBOS - VERBS

MENTIR
LIE

VERBOS - VERBS

ESCUCHAR
LISTEN

VERBOS - VERBS

MIRAR
LOOK

VERBOS - VERBS

BAJAR
LOWER

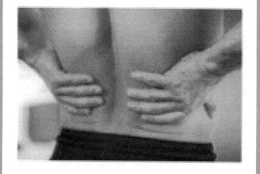

VERBOS - VERBS

CASARSE
MARRY

VERBOS - VERBS

COMPONER
MEND

VERBOS - VERBS

MOVER
MOVE

VERBOS - VERBS

NOTAR
NOTE

VERBOS - VERBS

NUMERAR
NUMBER

VERBOS - VERBS

OBLIGAR
OBLIGE

VERBOS - VERBS

OCUPAR

OCCUPY

VERBOS - VERBS

ABRIR

OPEN

VERBOS - VERBS

ORGANIZAR

ORGANIZE

VERBOS - VERBS

PINTAR

PAINT

VERBOS - VERBS

PERMITIR
PERMIT

VERBOS · VERBS

POSEER
POSSESS

VERBOS · VERBS

PREFERIR
PREFER

VERBOS · VERBS

PRESENTAR
PRESENT

VERBOS · VERBS

PROMETER
PROMISE

VERBOS - VERBS

TIRAR
PULL

VERBOS - VERBS

EMPUJAR
PUSH

VERBOS - VERBS

ALCANZAR
REACH

VERBOS - VERBS

Adriana Muñoz

REFERIR
REFER

VERBOS - VERBS

ALIVIAR
RELIEVE

VERBOS - VERBS

RECORDAR
REMEMBER

VERBOS - VERBS

QUITAR
REMOVE

VERBOS - VERBS

REPARAR
REPAIR

VERBOS - VERBS

REPLICAR
REPLY

VERBOS - VERBS

SUPLICAR
REQUEST

VERBOS - VERBS

DESCANSAR
REST

VERBOS - VERBS

Adriana Muñoz

PRECIPITARSE
RUSH

VERBOS - VERBS

AHORRAR
SAVE

VERBOS - VERBS

AFILAR
SHARPEN

VERBOS - VERBS

FIRMAR
SIGN

VERBOS - VERBS

FUMAR
SMOKE

VERBOS - VERBS

EMPEZAR
START

VERBOS - VERBS

ESTUDIAR
STUDY

VERBOS - VERBS

SUGERIR
SUGGEST

VERBOS - VERBS

SORPRENDER

SURPRISE

VERBOS - VERBS

DOMESTICAR

TAME

VERBOS - VERBS

CANSAR

TIRE

VERBOS - VERBS

PROBAR

TEST

VERBOS - VERBS

ATAR
TIE

VERBOS - VERBS

VIAJAR
TRAVEL

VERBOS - VERBS

CONFIAR
TRUST

VERBOS - VERBS

GIRAR
TURN

VERBOS - VERBS

USAR
USE

VERBOS - VERBS

VISITAR
VISIT

VERBOS - VERBS

ANDAR
WALK

VERBOS - VERBS

LAVAR
WASH

VERBOS - VERBS

PESAR
WEIGH

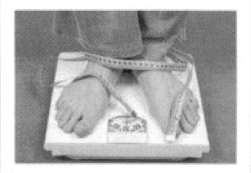

VERBOS - VERBS

TRABAJAR
WORK

VERBOS - VERBS

HERIR
WOUND

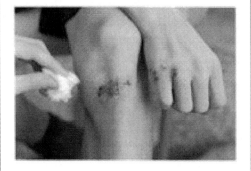

VERBOS - VERBS

¡HOLA!
HI!

FRASES - PHRASES

¡BUENOS DÍAS!

GOOD MORNING

FRASES - PHRASES

¡BUENAS TARDES!

GOOD AFTERNOON

FRASES - PHRASES

¡BUENAS NOCHES!

GOOD EVENING

FRASES - PHRASES

¿CÓMO ESTÁS?

HOW ARE YOU?
FORMAL: ¿CÓMO ESTÁ USTED?

FRASES - PHRASES

ADIÓS / CHAU

GOODBYE

FRASES - PHRASES

¡HASTA LUEGO!

LATER

FRASES - PHRASES

¡HASTA PRONTO!

SEE YOU SOON

FRASES - PHRASES

¡NOS VEMOS!

"SEE YA"

FRASES - PHRASES

¡HASTA LA VISTA!

UNTIL WE SEE EACH OTHER AGAIN

FRASES - PHRASES

ESTOY BIEN, GRACIAS!

I AM FINE, THANK YOU

FRASES - PHRASES

COMO SIEMPRE

AS ALWAYS

FRASES - PHRASES

GRACIAS

THANK YOU

FRASES - PHRASES

BIEN, GRACIAS
WELL, THANKS

MUY BIEN
VERY WELL

¿CÓMO TE VA?
HOW'S IT GOING?

¿CÓMO HAS IDO?
HOW'VE YOU BEEN?

¿QUÉ TAL?
WHAT'S UP?

FRASES - PHRASES

¿QUÉ PASA?
WHAT'S HAPPENING

FRASES - PHRASES

LO SIENTO
I'M SORRY

FRASES - PHRASES

NO SÉ
I DON'T KNOW

FRASES - PHRASES

TE AMO/TE QUIERO

I LOVE YOU

FRASES - PHRASES

TE EXTRAÑO

I MISS YOU

FRASES - PHRASES

NECESITO AYUDA

I NEED HELP

FRASES - PHRASES

¡BUENA SUERTE!

GOOD LUCK!

FRASES - PHRASES

¡DIVIÉRTETE!

HAVE FUN!

FRASES - PHRASES

¡CON MUCHO AMOR!

LOTS OF LOVE

FRASES - PHRASES

¡BUEN VIAJE!

HAVE A GOOD TRIP

FRASES - PHRASES

¡BUEN PROVECHO!

ENJOY YOUR MEAL

FRASES - PHRASES

¡SALUD!
CHEERS

FRASES - PHRASES

¡MUY BIEN!
WELL DONE!

FRASES - PHRASES

¡BUEN TRABAJO!
GOOD JOB!

FRASES - PHRASES

SÍ
YES

FRASES - PHRASES

NO
NO

FRASES - PHRASES

¡CUÍDATE!
TAKE CARE!

FRASES - PHRASES

¡BIENVENIDOS! / ¡BIENVENIDAS!
WELCOME!

FRASES - PHRASES

¡FELICITACIONES!
CONGRATULATIONS!

FRASES - PHRASES

LOS MEJORES DESEOS PARA ___
BEST WISHES TO ___

FRASES - PHRASES

¡FELIZ CUMPLEAÑOS!
HAPPY BIRTHDAY!

FRASES - PHRASES

¡PERDÓN!
EXCUSE ME!

FRASES - PHRASES

POR FAVOR
PLEASE

FRASES - PHRASES

¡NO SE PREOCUPE!
NO WORRIES

FRASES - PHRASES

¿PUEDE AYUDARME?
CAN YOU HELP ME?

FRASES - PHRASES

NO ENTIENDO
I DON'T UNDERSTAND

FRASES - PHRASES

¿COMO TE LLAMAS?
WHAT IS YOUR NAME?

FRASES - PHRASES

¿QUÉ HORA TIENES?

WHAT TIME IS IT?

ME LLAMO ___

MY NAME IS ___

CLARO QUE SÍ

OF COURSE

¿A QUÉ HORA ES EL DESAYNO?

WHAT TIME IS BREAKFAST?

ME GUSTÓ MUCHO LA COMIDA

I REALLY LIKED THE FOOD

FRASES - PHRASES

¿QUÉ RESTAURANTE ME RECOMIENDAS?

WHAT RESTAURANT DO YOU RECOMMEND?

FRASES - PHRASES

SABES CÓMO LLEGAR A...?

YOU KNOW HOW TO GET TO...?

FRASES - PHRASES

NECESITO UN TAXI/UBER, POR FAVOR

I NEED A TAXI/UBER PLEASE

FRASES - PHRASES

CLARO QUE NO
OF COURSE NOT

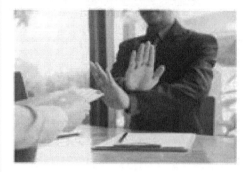

FRASES - PHRASES

A MI TAMBIÉN
ME TOO

FRASES - PHRASES

A MI TAMPOCO
ME NEITHER

FRASES - PHRASES

ESTOY BROMEANDO
I'M JUST KIDDING

FRASES - PHRASES

¿DÓNDE ESTÁ EL BAÑO?

WHERE IS THE BATHROOM

FRASES - PHRASES

¿PUEDO USAR EL BAÑO?

MAY I USE THE BATHROOM

FRASES - PHRASES

¿COMO ESTÁ EL TIEMPO?

HOW'S THE WEATHER

FRASES - PHRASES

¿CUÁNTO CUESTA?

HOW MUCH IS THIS?

FRASES - PHRASES

¿LISTO?

ARE YOU READY?

FRASES - PHRASES

¿VERDAD?

REALLY?

FRASES - PHRASES

¿QUÉ ES ESTO?

WHAT'S THIS?

FRASES - PHRASES

¡CALLETE!

SHUT UP!

FRASES - PHRASES

¡QUÉ LÁSTIMA!

WHAT A SHAME!

FRASES - PHRASES

¡TENGA CUIDADO!

BE CAREFUL!

FRASES - PHRASES

MUCHO GUSTO

NICE TO MEET YOU

FRASES - PHRASES

¿CUÁNDO...?

WHEN?

FRASES - PHRASES

¿POR QUÉ?

WHY?

FRASES - PHRASES

AQUÍ

HERE

FRASES - PHRASES

¿LO PODRÍA ESCRIBIR, POR FAVOR?

COULD YOU WRITE IT DOWN, PLEASE?

FRASES - PHRASES

HAY UN ERROR...

THERE'S A MISTAKE...

FRASES - PHRASES

¿DÓNDE ESTÁ...?

WHERE IS....?

FRASES - PHRASES

NO NECESITO ESO

I DON'T NEED THAT

FRASES - PHRASES

ES DEMASIADO CARO

IT'S TOO EXPENSIVE

FRASES - PHRASES

¿CUÁNTO CUESTA ESTO...?

HOW MUCH IS THIS?

FRASES - PHRASES

¿PODRÍA REPETIRLO, POR FAVOR?

COULD YOU REPEAT THAT, PLEASE?

FRASES - PHRASES

NO HABLO ESPAÑOL

I DON'T SPEAK ENGLISH

FRASES - PHRASES

ESTO ES MÍO

THIS IS MINE

FRASES - PHRASES

ESTO ES TUYO?

THIS IS YOURS?

FRASES - PHRASES

A LA IZQUIERDA

TO THE LEFT

FRASES - PHRASES

A LA DERECHA

TO THE RIGHT

FRASES - PHRASES

TENGO HAMBRE

I'M HUNGRY

FRASES - PHRASES

TENGO SED

I'M THIRSTY

FRASES - PHRASES

ESTOY HERIDO

I'M HURT

FRASES - PHRASES

ESTOY ENFERMO

I'M SICK

FRASES - PHRASES

ESTOY PERDIDO

I'M LOST

FRASES - PHRASES

TENGA CUIDADO

BE SAFE

FRASES - PHRASES

VOY A LLAMAR A LA POLICÍA

I'M GOING TO CALL THE COPS

FRASES - PHRASES

¿QUÉ TE GUSTA LEER?

WHAT DO YOU LIKE READING?

FRASES - PHRASES

¿QUE MÚSICA TE GUSTA?

WHAT KIND OF MUSIC DO YOU LIKE?

FRASES - PHRASES

MI FAVORITO ES...

MY FAVORITE ONE IS...

FRASES - PHRASES

ME GUSTA IR...

I LIKE TO GO TO...

FRASES - PHRASES

¿EN QUÉ TRABAJAS?

WHAT DO YOU DO FOR A LIVING?

FRASES - PHRASES

¿TE GUSTA TU TRABAJO?

DO YOU LIKE YOUR JOB?

FRASES - PHRASES

¿ME PUEDE AYUDAR CON ESTO?

CAN YOU HELP ME WITH THIS?

FRASES - PHRASES

¿PUEDO ENTRAR?

CAN I COME IN?

FRASES - PHRASES

¿QUIERES TOMAR UNA COPA?

WOULD YOU LIKE TO HAVE A DRINK?

FRASES - PHRASES

¿A DÓNDE DEBERÍAMOS IR A COMER?

WHERE SHOULD WE GO FOR LUNCH?

FRASES - PHRASES

¿ESTÁS LISTO?

ARE YOU READY?

FRASES - PHRASES

LLÁMAME CUANDO LLEGUES

CALL ME WHEN YOU ARRIVE

FRASES - PHRASES

ME VOY A CASA

I'M GOING HOME

FRASES - PHRASES

¡CUÁNTO TIEMPO SIN VERLO(A)!

LONG TIME NO SEE!

FRASES - PHRASES

QUÉ CUENTAS?

WHAT'S UP?

FRASES - PHRASES

¿QUÉ HAY DE NUEVO?

WHAT'S NEW?

FRASES - PHRASES

SOY SOLTERO(A).

I AM SINGLE.

FRASES - PHRASES

SOY ESTUDIANTE.

I'M A STUDENT.

FRASES - PHRASES

ESTOY JUBILADO/RETIRADO.

I AM RETIRED.

FRASES - PHRASES

ESTOY ESTUDIANDO ESPAÑOL.

I AM STUDYING SPANISH.

FRASES - PHRASES

SÓLO HABLO UN POCO.

I ONLY KNOW HOW TO TALK A LITTLE.

FRASES - PHRASES

PUEDO ESCRIBIR/ LEER/ HABLAR MUY BIEN.

I CAN WRITE/ READ/ SPEAK VERY WELL.

FRASES - PHRASES

ME GUSTA ESCUCHAR MÚSICA.

I ENJOY LISTENING TO MUSIC.

FRASES - PHRASES

Adriana Muñoz

ME GUSTAN LAS SERIES DE TERROR.

I LIKE HORROR SERIES.

FRASES - PHRASES

UNO DE MIS PASATIEMPOS ES ESCRIBIR.

ONE OF MY HOBBIES IS WRITING.

FRASES - PHRASES

ME ENCANTAN LOS LIBROS DE FANTASÍA.

I LOVE FANTASY BOOKS.

FRASES - PHRASES

TE GUSTARÍA IR CONMIGO?

WOULD YOU LIKE TO GO WITH ME?

FRASES - PHRASES

TE GUSTARÍA IR AL CINE MAÑANA?

WOULD YOU LIKE TO GO TO THE MOVIES TOMORROW?

FRASES - PHRASES

QUIERES TOMAR UN CAFÉ?

DO YOU WANT TO HAVE A COFFEE?

FRASES - PHRASES

TE GUSTARÍA SALIR CONMIGO?

WOULD YOU LIKE TO GO OUT WITH ME?

FRASES - PHRASES

ESTOY ESTRESADO(A).

I AM STRESSED OUT.

FRASES - PHRASES

ESTOY TRISTE.

I'M SAD.

FRASES - PHRASES

ESTOY MUY NERVIOSO(A).

I'M VERY NERVOUS.

FRASES - PHRASES

ESTOY FELIZ!

I AM HAPPY!

FRASES - PHRASES

ESTOY DECEPCIONADO.

I'M DISAPPOINTED.

FRASES - PHRASES

ME SIENTO MAL.

I FEEL BAD.

FRASES - PHRASES

TENGO MIEDO.

I AM AFRAID.

FRASES - PHRASES

NO TENGO NI IDEA DE QUÉ HACER.

I HAVE NO IDEA WHAT TO DO.

FRASES - PHRASES

ERES/ES MUY AMABLE.

YOU ARE VERY KIND.

FRASES - PHRASES

NOS TRAE LA CARTA, POR FAVOR?

WILL YOU BRING US THE MENU, PLEASE?

FRASES - PHRASES

QUÉ ME/NOS RECOMIENDA?

WHAT DO YOU RECOMMEND TO ME/US?

FRASES - PHRASES

VOY A TOMAR UN TÉ, GRACIAS.

I'LL HAVE SOME TEA, THANK YOU.

FRASES - PHRASES

NOS PUEDE TRAER LA CUENTA?

CAN YOU BRING US THE BILL?

FRASES - PHRASES

QUE QUIERES HACER HOY?

WHAT DO YOU WANT TO DO TODAY?

FRASES - PHRASES

DONDE SE ENCUENTRA LA ESTACIÓN DE SERVICIO?

WHERE IS THE GAS STATION LOCATED?

FRASES - PHRASES

DONDE PUEDO ENCONTRAR BICICLETAS?

WHERE CAN I FIND BICYCLES?

FRASES - PHRASES

ES SEGURO ANDAR POR LA NOCHE AQUÍ?

IS IT SAFE TO WALK AT NIGHT HERE?

FRASES - PHRASES

Adriana Muñoz

DONDE PUEDO
ENCONTRAR UNA FARMÁCIA?

WHERE CAN I FIND A PHARMACY?

FRASES - PHRASES

VA A LLOVER HOY?

WILL IT RAIN TODAY?

FRASES - PHRASES

DONDE PUEDO
ENCONTRAR UN TÁXI?

WHERE CAN I FIND A TAXI?

FRASES - PHRASES

PUEDE LLAMAR UN
TÁXI PARA MI/NOSOTROS?

CAN YOU CALL A TAXI FOR ME/US?

FRASES - PHRASES

INDEX - ÍNDICE

A

- Abandon - *Abandonar*.. 134
- Abolish - *Abolir*.. 168
- Absolve - *Absolver*.. 134
- Absorb - *Absorber*.. 168
- Abuse - *Injuriar*.. 134
- Accelerate - *Acelerar*.. 135
- Accent - *Acentuar*.. 169
- Accept - *Aceptar*.. 135
- Accuse - *Acusar*.. 169
- Accustom - *Acostumbrar*.. 135
- Achieve - *Conseguir*.. 169
- Acquire - *Adquirir*.. 135
- Act - *Actuar*.. 169
- Add - *Sumar*.. 136
- Admire - *Admirar*.. 136
- Admit - *Admitir*.. 170
- Adore - *Adorar*.. 136
- Advance - *Avanzar*.. 136
- Advertise - *Anunciar*.. 170
- Advise - *Aconsejar*.. 137
- Affirm - *Afirmar*.. 171
- Agree - *Acceder*.. 137
- Airplane - *Avión*.. 76
- Allow - *Permitir*.. 171
- Ambitious - *Ambicioso*.. 38
- American - *Estadounidense*.. 59
- Amount - *Ascender*.. 137
- Amuse / Have fun - *Divertir*.. 171
- Announce - *Anunciar*.. 137
- Annoy / Trouble - *Molestar*.. 166

- Answer - *Contestar*.. 138
- Ant - *Hormiga*.. 9
- Apologize - *Excusarse*.. 171
- Appear - *Aparecer*.. 138
- Apple - *Manzana*.. 17
- Appoint - *Nombrar*.. 172
- Approach - *Acercarse*.. 138
- Approve - *Aprobar*..172
- Are you ready? - *¿Listo?*.. 217
- Are you ready? - *¿Estás listo?*.. 226
- Arise - *Surgir/Levantarse*.. 96
- Armadillo - *Armadillo*.. 2
- Arrange - *Arreglar*.. 138
- Arrive - *Llegar*.. 145
- Art - *Arte*.. 73
- Artichokes - *Alcachofas*.. 29
- As always - *Como siempre*.. 204
- Ask - *Preguntar*.. 139
- Assure - *Asegurar*.. 172
- Astonish - *Asombrar*.. 139
- Attack - *Atacar*.. 172
- Attempt - *Intentar*.. 139
- Attend / Watch - *Asistir*.. 173
- Attract - *Atraer*.. 139
- Avoid - *Evitar*.. 173
- Awake - *Despertarse*.. 96

Adriana Muñoz

INDEX - ÍNDICE

B

- Bad / Mean / Evil - *Malo*.. 46
- Bagagge - *Bagaje*.. 69
- Balcony - *Balcón*.. 81
- Banana - *Banana*.. 18
- Bat - *Murciélago*..11
- Bathe - *Bañarse*.. 140
- Be / Am , Are, Is - *Ser / Estar*.. 96
- Be careful! - *¡Tenga Cuidado!*.. 218
- Be safe - *Tenga Cuidado*.. 223
- Beans - *Frijoles*.. 30
- Bear - *Oso*.. 11
- Bear - *Soportar*.. 97
- Beat / Hit / Strike - *Golpear*.. 97
- Became - *Llegar a Ser*.. 97
- Bed - *Cama*..71
- Bee - *Abeja*.. 1
- Beer - *Cerveza*.. 92
- Beet - *Remolacha*.. 31
- Beetle - *Escarabajo*.. 7
- Beg - *Rogar / Pedir*.. 173
- Begin - *Empezar*.. 97
- Believe - *Creer*.. 140
- Belong - *Pertenecer*.. 173
- Bend - *Doblar*.. 98
- Best wishes to - *Los mejores deseos para*.. 211
- Bet - *Apostar*.. 98
- Bicycle/Bike - *Bicicleta*.. 77
- Bid - *Pujar*.. 98
- Big - *Grande*.. 54
- Bind - *Atar*.. 98
- Bird - *Pájaro*.. 14
- Birthday - *Cumpleaños*.. 80
- Bite - *Morder*.. 99
- Black - *Negro*.. 34
- Blame - *Culpar*.. 140
- Bleed - *Sangrar*.. 99
- Blond - *Rubio*.. 56
- Blow - *Soplar*.. 99
- Blue - *Azul*.. 34
- Blueberry - *Arándano*.. 19
- Book - *Libro*.. 62
- Book - *Reservar*.. 174
- Boring - *Aburrido*.. 39
- Boy - *Niño*.. 82
- Brave - *Valiente*.. 39
- Brazilian - *Brasileño / a*.. 62
- Bread - *Pan*.. 86
- Break - *Romper*.. 99
- Breed - *Criar*.. 100
- Bring - *Traer / llevar*.. 100
- Broadcast - *Radiar*.. 100
- Broccoli - *Brócoli*.. 29
- Brown - *Marrón*.. 36
- Build - *Edificar*.. 100
- Bull - *Toro*.. 16
- Bumper - *Parachoques*.. 77
- Burn - *Quemar*.. 101
- Burst - *Reventar*.. 101
- Bus - *Autobús*.. 76
- Butter - *Mantequilla*.. 95

INDEX - ÍNDICE

- Butterfly - *Mariposa*.. 11
- Buy - *Comprar*.. 101
- Buzzard - *Buitre*.. 2

C

- Cab Driver - *Taxista*.. 85
- Cabbage - *Repollo*.. 29
- Cake - *Torta*.. 94
- Call me when you arrive - *Llámame cuando llegues*.. 227
- Camel - *Camello*.. 4
- Can - *Lata*.. 65
- Can I come in? - *¿Puedo entrar?*.. 226
- Can Opener - *Abrelatas*.. 69
- Can you bring us the bill? - *Nos puede traer la cuenta?*.. 234
- Can you call a taxi for me/us? - *Puede llamar un táxi para mi/nosotros?*.. 236
- Can you help me with this? - *¿Me puede ayudar con esto?*.. 225
- Can you help me? - *¿Puede ayudarme?*.. 212
- Canadian - *Canadiense*.. 58
- Candy - *Caramelo*.. 72
- Car - *Auto*.. 76
- Carambola - *Carambola*.. 22
- Carrot - *Zanahoria*.. 29
- Carry - *Llevar*.. 174
- Cash - *Cobrar*.. 140
- Cassava - *Yuca*.. 31
- Cast - *Arrojar*.. 101
- Cat - *Gato*.. 8
- Catch - *Coger*.. 102
- Cauliflower - *Coliflor*.. 28
- Cease - *Cesar*.. 174
- Celery - *Apio*.. 32
- Chair - *Silla*.. 83
- Change - *Cambiar*.. 141
- Chard - *Acelga*.. 27
- Charming - *Encantador*.. 42
- Cheap - *Barato*.. 50
- Check - *Comprobar*.. 174
- Cheers - *¡Salud!*.. 209
- cheese - *Queso*.. 86
- Cherry - *Cereza*.. 18
- Chestnut - *Castaña*.. 26
- Chicken - *Pollo*.. 12
- Chickpea - *Garbanzo*.. 31
- Childhood - *Niñez*.. 74
- Chinese - *Chino/a*.. 58
- Choose - *Elegir*.. 103
- City - *Ciudad*.. 75
- Claim - *Reclamar*.. 141
- Clean - *Limpiar*.. 175
- Clear - *Aclarar, Limpiar*.. 141
- Climb - *Trepar*.. 175
- Cling - *Agarrarse*.. 103
- Close - *Cerrar*.. 142
- Closet - *Guardarropa*.. 84
- Clothes - *Ropa*.. 75

INDEX - ÍNDICE

- Clumsy - *Torpe*.. 40
- Cockroach - *Cucaracha*.. 3
- Coconut - *Coco*.. 22
- Coffe - *Café*.. 62
- Coffee - *Café*.. 93
- Collect - *Recoger*.. 175
- Comb - *Peinar*.. 142
- Comb Hair - *Peine*.. 69
- Combine - *Combinar*.. 175
- Come - *Venir*.. 102
- Command - *Mandar*.. 142
- Commit - *Cometer*.. 176
- Compare - *Comparar*.. 145
- Complain - *Quejarse*.. 176
- Compose - *Componer*.. 143
- Conceal - *Ocultar*.. 176
- Condor - *Condor*.. 6
- Congratulations! - *¡Felicitaciones!*.. 210
- Consider - *Considerar*.. 143
- Consist - *Consistir*.. 176
- Contain - *Contener*.. 143
- Continue - *Continuar*.. 177
- Copy - *Copiar*.. 143
- Corn - *Choclo / Maíz*.. 33
- Correct - *Corregir*.. 177
- Cost - *Costar*.. 102
- Cough - *Toser*.. 144
- Could you repeat that, please? - *¿Podría repetirlo, por favor?*.. 221
- Could you write it down, please? - *¿Lo podría escribir, por favor?*.. 219
- Count - *Contar*.. 177
- Cover - *Cubrir*.. 144
- Cow - *Vaca*.. 16
- Crab - *Cangrejo*.. 5
- Craftsman - *Artesano*.. 74
- Cream Color - *Crema*.. 37
- Creep - *Arrastarse*.. 103
- Cross - *Cruzar*.. 177
- Crown - *Coronar*.. 144
- Cruel - *Cruel*.. 55
- Cucumber - *Pepino*.. 30
- Curmudgeon - *Cascarrabias*.. 49
- Cut - *Cortar*.. 102
- Cynical - *Cinico*.. 40

D

- Damage - *Dañar*.. 144
- Dance - *Bailar*.. 178
- Dark Skin - *Moreno*.. 57
- Dawn - *Amanecer*.. 145
- Deal - *Tratar*.. 103
- Deceive - *Engañar*.. 178
- Decide - *Decidir*.. 146
- Declare - *Declarar*.. 178
- Decorate - *Adornar*.. 170
- Deer - *Ciervo*.. 5
- Defend - *Defender*.. 146
- Deliver - *Entregar*.. 178
- Desire - *Desear*.. 146

INDEX - ÍNDICE

- Despise - *Despreciar*.. 179
- Destroy - *Destruir*.. 146
- Detach - *Separar*.. 179
- Develop - *Desarrollar*.. 147
- Devote - *Dedicar*.. 179
- Devour - *Devorar*.. 147
- Dig - *Cavar*.. 104
- Dirty - *Sucio*.. 52
- Discover - *Descubrir*.. 179
- Discreet / Quiet - *Discreto*.. 40
- Dislike - *Desaprobar*..147
- Disturb - *Perturbar*.. 180
- Divide - *Dividir*.. 147
- Do / Does - *Hacer*.. 104
- Do you like your job? - *¿Te gusta tu trabajo?*.. 225
- Do you want to have a coffee? - *Quieres tomar un café?*.. 231
- Dog - *Perro*.. 13
- Dolphin - *Delfín*.. 6
- Dominican Republic - *Dominicano / a*.. 61
- Donkey - *Burro*.. 3
- Door - *Puerta*.. 71
- Dove - *Paloma*.. 13
- Drag - *Arrastrar*.. 180
- Draw - *Dibujar*.. 104
- Dream - *Soñar*.. 104
- Drink - *Beber*.. 105
- Drive - *Conducir*.. 105
- Drive - *Dirigir*.. 170
- Drop - *Dejar Caer*..148
- Dry - *Secar*.. 180

E

- Eagle - *Águila*.. 1
- Earth - *Tierra*.. 83
- Eat - *Comer*.. 105
- Egg - *Huevo*.. 87
- Eggplant - *Berenjena*.. 27
- Elegant - *Elegante*.. 41
- Elephant - *Elefante*.. 7
- Employ - *Emplear*.. 145
- Emu - *Emú*.. 7
- Enclose - *Incluir*.. 180
- Encourage - *Animar*.. 145
- End - *Terminar*.. 181
- English - *Inglés / Inglesa*.. 60
- Enjoy - *Disfrutar*.. 148
- Enjoy your meal - *¡Buen provecho!*.. 208
- Enter - *Entrar*.. 181
- Entrepreneur - *Emprendedor*.. 42
- Establish - *Establecer*.. 148
- Esteem - *Estimar*.. 181
- Evoke - *Evocar*.. 148
- Exchange - *Cambiar*.. 181
- Excuse me! - *¡Perdón!*.. 211
- Expect / Wait - *Esperar*.. 149
- Experienced - *Experimentado*.. 42
- Explain - *Explicar*.. 182
- Explode - *Estallar*.. 149

INDEX - ÍNDICE

- Expose - *Exponer*.. 182
- Express - *Expresar*.. 149
- Extract - *Extraer*.. 182
- Eyes - *Ojos*.. 65

F

- Fail - *Fallar*.. 149
- Fall - *Caer*.. 105
- Fat - *Gordo*.. 56
- Feed - *Alimentar*.. 106
- Feel - *Sentir*.. 106
- Fetch - *Ir Por*.. 150
- Fig - *Higo*.. 19
- Fight - *Luchar*.. 106
- Fill - *Llenar*.. 182
- Find - *Encontrar*.. 106
- Fingers - *Dedos*.. 67
- Finish - *Acabar*.. 150
- Fish - *Pez*.. 13
- Fish - *Pescar*..183
- Fit - *Ajustar*.. 150
- Fix - *Fijar*.. 183
- Flamingo - *Flamenco*.. 7
- Flee - *Huir*.. 107
- Flip-flops - *Ojotas*.. 83
- Float - *Flotar*.. 150
- Flour - *Harina*.. 87
- Fly - *Volar*.. 107
- Fold - *Doblar*.. 183
- Follow - *Seguir*.. 151
- Forbid - *Prohibir*.. 107

- Forgive - *Perdonar*.. 108
- Forgot - *Olvidar*.. 107
- Fork - *Tenedor*.. 72
- Formal - *Formal*.. 43
- Found - *Fundar*.. 183
- Fox - *Zorro*.. 16
- Freeze - *Helar*.. 108
- French - *Francés / Francesa*.. 59
- Friday - *Viernes*.. 80
- Fridge - *Heladera*.. 81
- Fries / Potato Chips - *Papas Fritas*.. 90
- Frog - *Rana*.. 15
- Fun - *Divertido*.. 40
- Fur - *Pelaje*.. 74

G

- Gamble / Play - *Jugar*.. 184
- Garlic - *Ajo*.. 27
- Gather - *Recoger*.. 151
- Generous - *Generoso*.. 43
- Gentleman / Knight - *Caballero*.. 74
- German - *Alemán / Alemana*.. 58
- Get - *Obtener*.. 108
- Giraffe - *Jirafa*.. 10
- Girl - *Niña*.. 82
- Give - *Dar*.. 108
- Glasses - *Anteojo*..70
- Go / Goes - *Ir*.. 109
- Goat - *Chivo*.. 3
- Gold - *Dorado*.. 37

INDEX - ÍNDICE

- Good afternoon - *¡Buenas tardes!..* 202
- Good evening - *¡Buenas Noches!..* 202
- Good job! - *¡Buen trabajo!..* 209
- Good luck! - *¡Buena suerte!..* 207
- Good Morning - *¡Buenos días!..* 202
- Goodbye - *Adiós / Chau..* 203
- Govern - *Governar..* 184
- Grant - *Conceder..* 151
- Grapefruit - *Toronja..* 25
- Grapes - *Uvas..* 18
- Green - *Verde..* 35
- Greet - *Saludar..* 184
- Grey - *Gris..* 36
- Grind - *Moler..* 109
- Grow - *Crecer..* 109
- Guacamole - *Guacamole..* 96
- Guarana - *Guaraná..* 23
- Guard - *Guardar..* 151
- Guess - *Adivinar..* 184

H

- Hair - *Cabello..* 67
- Haitian - *Haitiano/a..* 59
- Ham - *Jamon..* 95
- Hamburger / Burger - *Hamburguesa..* 89
- Hammer - *Martillo..* 63
- Hand - *Mano..* 66
- Handle - *Manejar..* 152

- Handsome - *Guapo..* 53
- Hang - *Colgar..* 109
- Hang - *Ahorcar..* 185
- Happen - *Suceder..* 152
- Happy - *Feliz..* 53
- Happy birthday! - *¡Feliz Cumpleaños!..* 211
- Hare - *Liebre..* 10
- Hate - *Odiar..* 185
- Hateful - *Odioso..* 47
- Have - *Haber / Tener..* 110
- Have a good trip - *¡Buen viaje!..* 208
- Have fun! - *¡Diviértete!..* 208
- Hazelnut - *Avellana..* 26
- Head - *Cabeza..* 66
- Hear - *Oir..* 110
- Heart - *Corazón..* 84
- Heat - *Calentar..* 152
- Helicopter - *Helicóptero..* 77
- Help - *Ayudar..* 185
- Hen - *Gallina..* 8
- Here - *Aquí..* 219
- Hi! - *¡Hola!..* 201
- Hide - *Ocultar..* 110
- Hip - *Cadera..* 68
- Hippopotamus - *Hipopótamo..* 9
- Hire / Rent - *Alquilar..* 152
- Hold - *Agarrar..* 110
- Honest - *Sincero..* 51
- Honey - *Miel..* 88
- Honorable - *Noble..* 55

INDEX - ÍNDICE

- Horse - *Caballo*.. 4
- Hot - *Caliente*.. 53
- Hotdog - *Pancho / Perrito Caliente*.. 90
- How are you? Formal: ¿Cómo está usted? - *¿Cómo estás?*.. 202
- How much is this? - *¿Cuánto cuesta?*.. 216
- How much is this? - *¿Cuánto cuesta*.. 220
- How's it going? - *¿Cómo te va?*.. 205
- How's the weather - *¿Como está el tiempo?*.. 216
- How've you been? - *¿Cómo has ido?*.. 205
- Hummingbird - *Colibrí*.. 6
- Hunt - *Cazar*.. 153
- Hurry - *Apresurarse*.. 185
- Hurt - *Herir*.. 111

I

- I am afraid. - *Tengo miedo*.. 233
- I am fine, thank you - *Estoy bien, gracias!*.. 204
- I am happy! - *Estoy feliz!*.. 232
- I am retired - *Estoy jubilado/retirado*.. 228
- I am single. - *Soy soltero(a)...* 228
- I am stressed out. - *Estoy estresado(a)*.. 231
- I am studying Spanish. - *Estoy estudiando español*.. 229
- I can write/read/speak very well. - *Puedo escribir/leer/hablar muy bien*.. 229
- I don't need that - *No necesito eso*.. 220
- I don't know - *No sé*.. 206
- I don't speak english - *No hablo español*.. 221
- I don't understand - *No entiendo*.. 212
- I enjoy listening to music. - *Me gusta escuchar música*.. 229
- I feel bad. - *Me siento mal*.. 233
- I have no idea what to do. - *No tengo ni idea de qué hacer*.. 233
- I like horror series. - *Me gustan las series de terror*.. 230
- I like to go to... - *Me gusta ir*.. 225
- I love fantasy books. - *Me encantan los libros de fantasía*.. 230
- I love you - *Te amo/Te quiero*.. 207
- I mis you - *Te extraño*.. 207
- I need a taxi/uber please - *Necesito un taxi/uber, por favor*.. 214
- I need help - *Necesito ayuda*.. 207
- I only know how to talk a little. - *Sólo hablo un poco*.. 229
- I really liked the food - *Me gustó mucho la comida*.. 214

INDEX - ÍNDICE

- I'll have some tea, thank you. - *Voy a tomar un té, gracias*.. 234
- I'm a student. - *Soy estudiante*.. 228
- I'm disappointed. - *Estoy decepcionado*.. 232
- I'm going home - *Me voy a casa*.. 227
- I'm going to call the cops - *Voy a llamar a la policía*.. 224
- I'm hungry - *Tengo hambre*.. 222
- I'm hurt - *Estoy herido*.. 223
- I'm just kidding - *Estoy bromeando*.. 215
- I'm lost - *Estoy perdido*.. 223
- I'm sad. - *Estoy triste*.. 232
- I'm sick - *Estoy enfermo*.. 223
- I'm sorry - *Lo siento*.. 206
- I'm thirsty - *Tengo sed*.. 222
- I'm very nervous. - *Estoy muy nervioso(a)*.. 232
- Imagine - *Imaginar*.. 153
- Immature - *Inmadura*.. 44
- Impatient - *Impaciente*.. 44
- Imply - *Implicar*.. 186
- Import - *Importar*.. 153
- Impress - *Impresionar*.. 186
- Improve - *Mejorar*.. 153
- Impulsive - *Impulsivo*.. 44
- Include - *Incluir*.. 186
- Increase - *Aumentar*.. 154
- Inquire - *Averiguar*.. 186
- Intend - *Proponerse*.. 154
- Interesting - *Interesante*.. 45
- Intolerant / Illiberal - *Intolerante*.. 45
- Invent - *Inventar*.. 187
- Invite - *Invitar*.. 154
- Iron - *Planchar*.. 187
- Is it safe to walk at night here? - *Es seguro andar por la noche aquí?*.. 235
- Island - *Isla*.. 64
- It's too expensive - *Es demasiado caro*.. 220
- Italian - *Italiano / a*.. 60

J

- Jackfruit - *Yaca/Jaca*.. 21
- Jam - *Mermelada*.. 88
- Jamaican - *Jamaicano / a*.. 60
- Japanese - *Japonés / Japonesa*.. 60
- Jealous - *Celoso*.. 39
- Join / Unite - *Unir*.. 154
- Joke - *Bromear*..187
- Juice - *Jugo*.. 94
- Jump - *Saltar*.. 155
- Justify - *Justificar*.. 187

INDEX - ÍNDICE

K

- Kangaroo - *Canguro*.. 4
- Keep - *Conservar*.. 111
- Kernels - *Almendra*.. 25
- Kick - *Cocear*.. 155
- Kill - *Matar*.. 188
- Kind - *Amable*.. 38
- Kiss - *Besar*.. 155
- Kiwi - *Kiwi*.. 23
- Kneel - *Arrodillarse*.. 111
- Knife - *Cuchillo*.. 71
- Knit - *Hacer Punto*.. 112
- Know - *Saber / Conocer*.. 111

L

- Land - *Aterrizar*.. 155
- Language - *Idioma*.. 78
- Last - *Durar*.. 188
- Later - *¡Hasta luego!*.. 203
- Laugh - *Reír*.. 156
- Lay - *Poner*.. 112
- Lazy - *Perezoso*.. 48
- Lead - *Conducir*.. 112
- Leaf - *Hojas*.. 71
- Lean - *Apoyarse*.. 112
- Leap - *Brincar*.. 113
- Learn - *Aprender*.. 113
- Leave - *Dejar*.. 113
- Lemon - *Limón*.. 18
- Lend - *Prestar*.. 113
- Leon - *León*.. 10

- Let - *Permitir*.. 114
- Letter - *Carta*.. 85
- letters - *Letras*.. 63
- Lettuce - *Lechuga*.. 30
- Lie - *Echarse*.. 114 , *Mentir*.. 188
- Lifeguard - *Salvavidas*.. 70
- Light - *Encender*.. 114
- Light Brown - *Beige*.. 35
- Like - *Gustar*.. 156
- Lime - *Lima*.. 24
- Listen - *Escuchar*.. 188
- Live - *Vivir*.. 156
- Llama - *Llama*.. 10
- Long time no see! - *¡Cuánto tiempo sin verlo(a)!*.. 227
- Look - *Mirar*.. 189
- Lose - *Perder*.. 114
- Lots of love - *¡Con mucho amor!*.. 208
- Love - *Amor*.. 86
- Love - *Amar*.. 156
- Lower - *Bajar*.. 189
- Luggage - *Equipaje*.. 85
- Lychee - *Lichi*.. 23

M

- Maintain / Keep - *Mantener*.. 157
- Make - *Hacer*.. 115
- Man Hombres: Men - *Hombre*.. 75
- Mango - *Mango*.. 21
- Map - *Mapa*.. 78

INDEX - ÍNDICE

- Marry - *Casarse*.. 189
- Maticulous - *Meticuloso*.. 46
- May I use the bathroom - *¿Puedo usar el baño?*.. 216
- Me neither - *A mi tampoco*.. 215
- Me too - *A mi también*.. 215
- Mean - *Significar*.. 115
- Measure - *Medir*.. 157
- Meat - *Carne*.. 92
- Meat / Beef - *Bife*.. 92
- Meddling - *Entrometido*.. 45
- Meet - *Encontrar*.. 115
- Melon - *Melón*.. 20
- Mend - *Componer*.. 189
- Mention - *Mencionar*.. 157
- Messages - *Mensajes*.. 63
- Mexican - *Mexicano / a*.. 61
- Milk - *Leche*.. 93
- Milkshake - *El Batido*..94
- Mistake - *Equivocar*.. 115
- Monday - *Lunes*.. 79
- Monkey - *Mono*.. 11
- Moody - *Malhumurado*.. 46
- Mouse - *Ratón*.. 14
- Mouth - *Boca*.. 67
- Move - *Mover*.. 190
- Musician - *Músico*.. 64
- My favorite one is... - *Mi favorito es*.. 224
- My name is ___ - *Me llamo ___*.. 213

N

- Nachos - *Nachos*.. 91
- Nails - *Uñas*.. 68
- Naive - *Ingenuo*.. 45
- Name - *Nombrar*.. 157
- Naughty - *Travieso*.. 52
- Neck - *Cuello*.. 66
- Nectarine - *Nectarina*.. 24
- Nervous - *Nervioso*.. 47
- New - *Nuevo*.. 57
- Nice / Friendly - *Simpático*.. 51
- Nice to meet you - *Mucho gusto*.. 218
- Nightingale - *Ruiseñor*.. 14
- No - *No*.. 210
- No worries - *¡No se preocupe!*.. 212
- Nose - *Nariz*.. 67
- Note - *Notar*.. 190
- Notice - *Notar*.. 158
- Number - *Numerar*.. 190
- Nuts - *Frutos Secos*.. 25

O

- Oat - *Avena*.. 89
- Obey - *Obedecer*.. 158
- Oblige - *Obligar*.. 158, 190
- Occupy - *Ocupar*.. 191
- Odd - *Raro*.. 58
- Of course - *Claro que sí*.. 213
- Of course not - *Claro que no*.. 215
- Offer - *Ofrecer*.. 158

INDEX - ÍNDICE

- Old - *Viejo*.. 57
- Olive - *Aceituna*.. 19
- Olive Oil - *Azeite de Oliva*.. 95
- One of my hobbies is writing. - *Uno de mis pasatiempos es escribir*... 230
- Onion - *Cebolla*.. 30
- Open - *Abrir*.. 191
- Orange - *Naranja*.. 19
- Orange - *Naranja*.. 37
- Order - *Ordenar*.. 159
- Organize - *Organizar*.. 191
- Oven - *Horno*.. 81
- Overcome - *Vencer*.. 116
- Owl - *Búho/Lechuza*.. 3
- Ox - *Buey*.. 2

P

- Pack - *Empaquetar*.. 159
- Paint - *Pintar*.. 191
- Papaya - *Papaya*.. 24
- Paprika - *Pimentón*.. 32
- Parrot - *Papagayo*.. 14
- Parsley - *Perejil*.. 28
- Pass - *Pasar*.. 159
- Passion fruit - *Chinola*.. 20
- Pasta - *Pasta*.. 87
- Patient - *Paciente*..47
- Pay - *Pagar*.. 116
- Peach - *Durazno*.. 16
- Pear - *Pera*.. 17
- Peas - *Arvejas*.. 33
- Pen - *Bolígrafo*.. 85
- Pencil - *Lápis*.. 82
- Penguin - *Pingüino*.. 12
- Pepper - *Pimienta*.. 27
- Permit - *Permitir*.. 192
- Pernickety - *Quisquilloso*.. 42
- Persimmon - *Caqui*.. 22
- Persistent - *Perseverante*.. 48
- Petty - *Mezquino*.. 47
- Phone - *Teléfono*.. 73
- Pig - *Cerdo*.. 5
- Pine nut - *Piñon*.. 26
- Pineapple - *Piña*.. 21
- Pink - Rosa / *Rosado*.. 36
- Pistachio - *Pistacho*.. 26
- Pitaya - *Pitaya*.. 21
- Pizza - *Pizza*.. 89
- Place - *Colocar*.. 159
- Planet - *Planeta*.. 78
- Please - *Agradar*.. 160
- Please - *Por favor*.. 211
- Plum - *Ciruela*.. 17
- Polite - *Educado*.. 41
- Polite - *Cortés*.. 54
- Pomegranate - *Granada*.. 20
- Popcorn - *Palomitas*.. 91
- Porcupine - *Puerco Espín*.. 12
- Portuguese - *Portugués / Portuguesa*.. 62
- Possess - *Poseer*.. 192

INDEX - ÍNDICE

- Potato - *Patata / Papas*.. 31
- Practise - *Practicar*.. 160
- Prefer - *Preferir*.. 192
- Prepare - *Preparar*.. 160
- Present - *Presentar*.. 192
- Pretentious - *Pretencioso*.. 48
- Produce - *Producir*.. 160
- Promise - *Prometer*.. 193
- Prompt - *Puntual*.. 48
- Propose - *Proponer*.. 161
- Provocateur - *Provocador*.. 49
- Prudent - *Prudente*.. 49
- Puerto Rican - *Puertorriqueño / a*.. 61
- Pull - *Tirar*.. 193
- Pumpkin - *Calabaza*.. 32
- Punish - *Castigar*.. 161
- Purple - *Lila*.. 36
- Push - *Empujar*.. 193
- Put - *Poner*.. 116
- Puzzle - *Rompecabezas*.. 70
- Rabbit - *Conejo*.. 6
- Rain - *Llover*.. 161
- Raspberry - *Frambuesa*.. 20
- Reach - *Alcanzar*.. 193
- Read - *Leer*.. 116
- Really? - *¿Verdad?*.. 217
- Receive - *Recibir*.. 161
- Red - *Rojo*.. 34
- Refer - *Referir*.. 194
- Refuse - *Rehusar*.. 162

- Relieve - *Aliviar*.. 194
- Remain - *Permanecer*.. 162
- Remember - *Recordar*.. 194
- Remind - *Recordar*.. 162
- Remove - *Quitar*.. 194
- Rent - *Arrendar*.. 162
- Repair - *Reparar*.. 195
- Repeat - *Repetir*.. 163
- Reply - *Replicar*.. 195
- Report - *Informar*.. 163
- Request - *Suplicar*.. 195
- Require - *Requerir*.. 163
- Responsible - *Responsable*.. 49
- Rest - *Descansar*.. 195
- Return - *Volver*.. 163
- Ride - *Montar*.. 117
- Ridiculous - *Ridículo*.. 50
- Ring / Call - *Llamar*.. 117
- Rise - *Arroz*.. 87, *Levantarse*.. 117
- Rogue / Naughty - *Pícaro*.. 46
- Rooster - *Gallo*.. 8
- Rubber - *Goma*.. 86
- Rude - *Maleducado*.. 43
- Run - *Correr*.. 117
- Rush - *Precipitarse*.. 196
- Russian - *Ruso / a*.. 61

INDEX - ÍNDICE

S

- Sad - *Triste*.. 52
- Safe - *Seguro*.. 50
- Sail - *Navegar*.. 164
- Salad - *Ensalada*.. 90
- Salt - *Sal*.. 88
- Sandwich - *Sándwiches*.. 91
- Sardine - *Sardina*.. 15
- Saturday - *Sábado*.. 80
- Save - *Ahorrar*.. 196
- Say - *Decir*.. 118
- School - *Colegio*.. 64
- Scissors - *Tijera*.. 82
- Seagull - *Gaviota*.. 9
- See - *Ver*.. 118
- See ya - *¡Nos vemos!*.. 203
- See you soon - *¡Hasta Pronto!*.. 203
- Seek - *Buscar*.. 118
- Seem - *Parecer*.. 164
- Selfish - *Egoísta*.. 41
- Sell - *Vender*.. 118
- Send - *Enviar*.. 119
- Sensitive - *Sensible*.. 51
- Set - *Poner (se)*.. 119
- Sew - *Coser*.. 119
- Shake - *Sacudir*.. 119
- Shallow Person - *Superficial*.. 52
- Sharpen - *Afilar*.. 196
- Shear - *Esquilar*.. 120
- Sheep - *Oveja*.. 12
- Shine - *Brillar*.. 120
- Shoes - *Zapato*.. 84
- Shoot - *Disparar*.. 120
- Shout - *Gritar*.. 164
- Show - *Mostrar*.. 120
- Shower - *Ducha*.. 81
- Shrink - *Encogerse*.. 121
- Shut - *Cerrar*.. 121
- Shut up! - *¡Callete!*.. 217
- Shy - *Tímido*.. 53
- Sidra - *Sidra*.. 23
- Sign - *Firmar*.. 196
- Silver - *Plateado*.. 37
- Simple - *Simple*.. 57
- Sing - *Cantar*.. 121
- Sink - *Hundir*.. 121
- Sit - *Sentarse*.. 122
- Skillful - *Hábil*.. 44
- Skin - *Piel*.. 68
- Skinny - *Flaco*.. 56
- Sky Blue - *Celeste*.. 35
- Skyscrapers - *Rascacielos*.. 83
- Sleep - *Dormir*.. 122
- Slide - *Resbalar*.. 122
- Small - *Pequeño*.. 54
- Smell - *Oler*.. 122
- Smile - *Sonreír*.. 164
- Smoke - *Fumar*.. 197
- Smug - *Engreído*.. 39
- Snack - *Bocadillo*.. 92
- Soft Drinks - *Resfrescos*.. 93
- Soldier - *Soldado*.. 64

INDEX - ÍNDICE

- Sound - *Sonar*.. 165
- Soup - *Sopa*.. 90
- Soursop - *Guanabana*.. 22
- Sow - *Sembrar*.. 123
- Spanish - *Español / Española*.. 59
- Speak / Talk - *Hablar*.. 123
- Speed - *Acelerar*.. 123
- Spell - *Deletrear*.. 123
- Spend - *Gastar*.. 124
- Spider - *Araña*.. 1
- Spill - *Derramar*.. 124
- Spin - *Hilar*.. 124
- Spinach - *Espinaca*.. 33
- Spit - *Escupir*.. 124
- Split - *Hender / Partir / Rajar*.. 125
- Spoil - *Entropear*.. 125
- Spoon - *Cuchara*.. 72
- Spread - *Extender*.. 125
- Spring - *Saltar*.. 125
- Squirrel - *Ardilla*.. 1
- Stand - *Estar en Pie*.. 126
- Star - *Estrella*.. 63
- Start - *Empezar*.. 197
- Steal - *Robar*.. 126
- Stick - *Pegar / Engomar*.. 126
- Sting - *Picar*.. 126
- Stink - *Apestar*.. 127
- Stop - *Parar*.. 165
- Stork - *Cigüeña*.. 4
- Stride - *Dar Zancadas*.. 127
- Strong - *Duro*.. 50, *Fuerte*.. 54

- Study - *Estudiar*.. 197
- Subway - *Metro*.. 77
- Sugar - *Azúcar*.. 88
- Suggest - *Sugerir*.. 197
- Sunday - *Domingo*.. 80
- Suppose - *Suponer*.. 165
- Surprise - *Sorprender*.. 198
- Swallow - *Golondrina*.. 8
- Swear - *Jurar*.. 127
- Sweat - *Sudar*.. 127
- Sweep - *Barrer*.. 128
- Sweet - *Dulce*.. 41
- Swell - *Hinchar*.. 128
- Swim - *Nadar*.. 128
- Swing - *Columpiarse*.. 128

T

- Tacos - *Tacos*.. 91
- Take - *Coger*.. 129
- Take care! - *¡Cuídate!*.. 210
- Tamarind - *Tamarindo*.. 24
- Tame - *Domesticar*.. 198
- Taste / Try - *Probar*.. 165
- Tea - *Té*.. 94
- Teach - *Enseñar*.. 129
- Tear - *Rasgar*.. 129
- Tell - *Decir*.. 129
- Test - *Probar*.. 198
- Thank - *Agradecer*.. 166
- Thank you - *Gracias*.. 204

INDEX - ÍNDICE

- There's a mistake... - *Hay un error..* 219
- Think - *Pensar..* 130
- This is mine - *Esto es mío..* 221
- This is yours? - *Esto es tuyo?..* 221
- Throw - *Arronjar / Tirar..* 130
- Thrust - *Introducir..* 130
- Thursday - *Jueves..* 79
- Tie - *Atar..* 199
- Tire - *Cansar..* 198
- To the left - *A la Izquierda..* 222
- To the right - *A la derecha..* 222
- Toad - *Sapo..* 15
- Toe - *Pie..* 66
- Tomato - *Tomate..* 28
- Tool - *Herramienta..* 73
- Toothbrush - *Cepillo De Dientes..* 69
- Touch - *Tocar..* 166
- Translate - *Traducir..* 166
- Travel - *Viajar..* 199
- Tread - *Pisar / Hollar..* 130
- Trip - *Viaje..* 84
- Truck - *Camión..* 76
- Trust - *Confiar..* 199
- Tuesday - *Martes..* 79
- Turkey - *Pavo..* 13
- Turn - *Girar..* 199
- Turtle - *Tortuga..* 15

U
- Ugly - *Feo..* 53
- Umbrella - *Paraguas..* 70
- Undergo - *Suffer / Sufrir..* 131
- Understand - *Entender..* 131
- Undertake - *Emprender..* 131
- Unsociable - *Huraño..* 38
- Until we see each other again - *¡Hasta la vista!..* 204
- Use - *Usar..* 200

V
- Vain - *Vanidoso..* 55
- Vary - *Variar..* 167
- Very well - *Muy bien..* 205
- Violet - *Morado..* 35
- Visit - *Visitar..* 200

W
- Waist - *Cintura..* 68
- Wake - *Despertarse..* 131
- Walk - *Andar..* 200
- Walnut - *Nuez..* 25
- Want - *Querer..* 167
- Warm / Loving - *Afectuoso..* 38
- Wash - *Lavar..* 200
- Watch - *Vigilar..* 167
- Water - *Agua..* 73, 93
- Watercress - *Berro..* 32
- Watermelon - *Sandía..* 17
- Weak - *Débil..* 43, 55

INDEX - ÍNDICE

- Wear - *Ponerse*..132
- Weather - *Clima*.. 78
- Weave - *Tejer*.. 132
- Wednesday - *Miércoles*.. 79
- Weep / Cry - *Llorar*.. 132
- Weigh - *Pesar*.. 201
- Welcome! - *¡Bienvenidos! / ¡Bienvenidas!*.. 210
- Well done! - *¡Muy bien!*.. 209
- Well, thanks - *Bien, gracias*.. 205
- Wet - *Mojar*.. 132
- Whale - *Ballena*.. 2
- What a shame! - *¡Qué lástima!*.. 218
- What do you do for a - *¿En qué trabajas?*.. 225
- What do you like reading? - *¿Qué te gusta leer?*.. 224
- What do you recommend to me/us? - *Qué me/nos recomienda?*.. 234
- What do you want to do today? - *Que quieres hacer hoy?*.. 235
- What is your name? - *¿Como te llamas?*.. 212
- What kind of music do you like? - *¿Que música te gusta?*.. 224
- What restaurant do you recommend? - *¿Qué restaurante me recomiendas?*.. 214
- what time is breakfast? - *¿A qué hora es el desayno?*..213
- What time is it? - *¿Qué hora tienes?*.. 213
- What's happening - *¿Qué pasa?*.. 206
- What's new? - *¿Qué hay de nuevo?*.. 228
- What's this? - *¿Qué es esto?*.. 217
- What's up? - *¿Qué tal?*.. 206, *Qué cuentas?*..227
- Wheel - *Rueda*.. 72
- When? - *¿Cuándo...?*.. 218
- where can I find a pharmacy? - *Donde puedo encontrar una farmácia?*.. 236
- Where can I find a taxi? - *donde puedo encontrar un táxi?*.. 236
- Where can I find bicycles? - *Donde puedo encontrar bicicletas?*.. 235
- Where is the bathroom - *¿Dónde está el baño?*.. 216
- Where is the gas station located? - *Donde se encuentra la estación de servicio?*.. 235
- Where is....? - *¿Dónde está...?*.. 220
- Where should we go for lunch? - *¿A dónde deberíamos ir a comer?*.. 226
- White - *Blanco*.. 33
- Why? - *¿Por qué?*.. 219
- Wild boar - *Jabalí*.. 9
- Wildlife - *Fauna*.. 65

INDEX - ÍNDICE

- Will it rain today? - *va a llover hoy?*.. 236
- Will you bring us the menu, please? - *Nos trae la carta, por favor?*.. 234
- Win / Earn / Gain - *Ganar*.. 133
- Wind - *Enrollar*.. 133
- Wine - *Vino*.. 95
- Wise / Rational - *Sensato*.. 51
- Wish - *Desear*.. 167
- Withdraw - *Retirarse*.. 133
- Woman Mujeres: Women - *Mujer*.. 75
- Woods - *Bosque*.. 65
- Work - *Trabajar*.. 201
- Worry - *Preocuparse*.. 168
- Would you like to go out with me? - *Te gustaría salir conmigo?*.. 231
- Would you like to go to the movies tomorrow? - *Te gustaría ir al cine mañana?*.. 231
- Would you like to go with me? - *Te gustaría ir conmigo?*.. 230
- Would you like to have a drink? - *¿Quieres tomar una copa?*.. 226
- Wound - *Herir*.. 201
- Wring - *Torcer*.. 133
- Write - *Escribir*.. 134

Y
- Yellow - *Amarillo*.. 34
- Yes - *Sí*.. 209
- Yogurt - *Yogur*.. 89
- You are very kind. - *Eres/Es muy amable*... 233
- you know how to get to...? - *¿Sabes cómo llegar a...?*.. 214

Z
- Zebra - *Cebra*.. 5
- Zucchini - *Calabacín*.. 28

AUTHOR BIO

Adriana Muñoz loves languages.

As a Spanish-American, she served as a linguist for six years in the United States Navy before continuing her language proficiencies by teaching others who want to learn them as a second language or improve on their native tongue.

She's fluent in Spanish, Portuguese, French, English, and Arabic.

Adrian grew up in Spain and now resides in America with her family, and publishes language learning books to help those traveling or just wanting to learn another language.

Made in the USA
Las Vegas, NV
24 March 2023